DUNKIRK

by
CHRISTOPHER NOLAN

Storyboards drawn by
RICHARD BENNETT

D0001638

FABER & FABER

First published in 2017
by Faber & Faber Limited
Bloomsbury House
74–77 Great Russell Street
London WC1B 3DA

Typeset by Country Setting, Kingsdown, Kent CT14 8ES
Printed annd bound in the UK by CPI Group (UK) Ltd, Croydon CR0 4YY

The right of Christopher Nolan to be identified
as author of this work has been asserted in accordance with
Section 77 of the Copyright, Designs and Patents Act 1988

Storyboards drawn by Richard Bennett

A CIP record for this book is available from the British Library

ISBN 978-0-571-33625-8

2 4 6 8 10 9 7 5 3

Contents

Warner Bros. Pictures
presentation

A Syncopy
production

A Film by
CHRISTOPHER NOLAN

Dunkirk

FIONN WHITEHEAD
TOM GLYNN-CARNEY
JACK LOWDEN
HARRY STYLES
ANEURIN BARNARD
JAMES D'ARCY
BARRY KEOGHAN

with
KENNETH BRANAGH
CILLIAN MURPHY
MARK RYLANCE
and
TOM HARDY

Written and Directed by	CHRISTOPHER NOLAN
Produced by	EMMA THOMAS, P.G.A.
Produced by	CHRISTOPHER NOLAN, P.G.A.
Executive Producer	JAKE MYERS
Director of Photography	HOYTE VAN HOYTEMA, ASC, FSF, NSC
Production Designer	NATHAN CROWLEY
Edited by	LEE SMITH, ACE
Music by	HANS ZIMMER
Visual Effects Supervisor	ANDREW JACKSON
Special Effects Supervisor	SCOTT FISHER
Costume Designer	JEFFREY KURLAND
Casting by	JOHN PAPSIDERA, CSA
	TOBY WHALE, CDG

Allowing Fate to be Arbitrary

A conversation between
Christopher Nolan and Jonathan Nolan

JONATHAN NOLAN   What made you want to make a war movie?

CHRISTOPHER NOLAN   I never wanted to make a war movie. In a funny sort of way, I don't see *Dunkirk* as a war movie at all. I think the reason I was drawn to the story of Dunkirk is because it's a survival story. I wouldn't feel comfortable doing what I consider to be a war movie, never having fought in a war.
    You always feel a bit fraudulent as a filmmaker. I would feel truly fraudulent. Whereas a survival story, I can tap into that emotion. Dunkirk as a survival story, as a sort of ticking-clock suspense story, I feel confident and comfortable taking that on. I don't know how people who haven't been in a war take on a war movie. I think that would be daunting.

JONATHAN   Well, they'd probably find their way back to the original material. You'd find someone who's written on the topic, who connects you to it, I guess. As a writer, you pride yourself on being able to imagine yourself in situations, but this does feel like the one that is maybe beyond the bounds.

CHRISTOPHER   The last time I looked at The *Thin Red Line* on Bluray – it's a favorite movie of mine, as you know – and included in the Criterion Edition is an essay by James Jones who wrote the novel. He's talking about war movies – and he just shreds them all.

JONATHAN   (*Laughter.*)

CHRISTOPHER   I mean, literally just shreds them. He basically says, since *All Quiet on the Western Front*, what has there been to say about war? That war turns men into animals; the longer

ix

they're in it, the more they turn into animals. That's it, that's all there is to say about it. He then goes through all the different story models – such as the benevolent sergeant; he goes through all the things and just shreds them, as someone who's been in war. I found what he said quite sobering because I was about to start writing the script. It really spoke to things that I've worried about. You've got to talk to people who were really in it, who've been through these things.

JONATHAN   Did you spend a lot of time doing research and talking to people?

CHRISTOPHER   I did a lot of reading of first-hand accounts. And partly inspired by James Jones, I then watched *All Quiet on the Western Front*, which I don't think I'd ever seen.

JONATHAN   I haven't seen it.

CHRISTOPHER   They did a silent version and then they also released a sound version, because it's right on the transition from silent cinema. I'd seen bits of it when I was a kid. It's got these amazing camera moves of the silent era, before it all became very static, but it does have sound. And it's absolutely relentless. They've got a shelling scene where they're in the trenches and it just goes on so much longer than you can imagine, more than you can take. And, when I got to the end, I was like, wow, this pretty much says it all – as far as the horror of war goes. And there's a nod to that film at the beginning of *Dunkirk* with Gibson taking the boots off the body, and then tying his boots – there's a whole thing about boots in *All Quiet on the Western Front*.

JONATHAN   Right.

CHRISTOPHER   I moved on from there and said, okay, I really have to address this as a survival story, something that I can tap into and relate to. And that's why the enemy is unseen. I try to get across the experience that I got from reading first-hand accounts – the point of view of somebody on the beach, who didn't really see the enemy very much. They're threatened by the planes, they're threatened by the bombs and the unknown enemy, which I think is terrifying.

JONATHAN At what point in the process did that idea occur – the idea that you would never see the enemy, not until the last shot, out of focus. You would feel them. I'm trying to remember, when I watched the movie for the first time, if I even noticed, because the tension is so effective.

CHRISTOPHER People tend not to, actually.

JONATHAN Yeah, you had to point it out to me, which I thought was great. At what point when you were writing the script did you decide, or was it more organic?

CHRISTOPHER I honestly can't remember. I clearly must have decided. I remember deciding very clearly that I didn't want the generals in the rooms, I didn't want Churchill, I didn't want maps, I didn't want too much knowledge. I found this way of having them overhear some knowledge, from the guys on the mole. It was sort of an attempt to give you just enough that you understand what's going on but not too much, so you only have the level of knowledge of the soldier. I remember deciding that because I was looking at films like *A Bridge Too Far*, which is such a brilliant film.

JONATHAN A great film.

CHRISTOPHER But every time they cut to the generals in the rooms, I lose interest. I'm seeing the German High Command, I'm seeing the Luftwaffe. It takes me out of the experience.

JONATHAN It also suggests a level of sort of omniscience and awareness for those people that wasn't accurate to what is actually happening.

CHRISTOPHER Exactly. And it dated the films, because there was a particular way that those World War Two films were made when we were kids. Actually, they were made before we were kids, but they were the ones we grew up with, watching them on TV on Sunday. All these movies had a particular formula that involved the higher-up generals – there's a version of that in contemporary cinema: the control room with all the monitors and everything. But it's not even quite as codified in the same way. There was a real rhythm of 'you're in it' – a cinematic rhythm – and then you get pulled out of it to the kind of higher-ups drinking champagne in the Schloss and talking about whatever. And it dates the films, they're hard to relate to now. Just as a rhythm. What I'm interested in in movies right now is where movies are firing on all cylinders – the subjective experience going through it.

JONATHAN   Trapping you.

CHRISTOPHER   So I think not seeing the Germans evolved naturally out of that. But the thing that I do remember is in the dialogue and in the text and in the cards and stuff to begin with, there was much talking about Nazis, the characters were always talking about Nazis, reminding the contemporary audience how awful this conflict was, how evil the bad guys were.

JONATHAN   Right.

CHRISTOPHER   When Mark Rylance read the script – I wanted him to play Dawson – I had told him this whole thing about not seeing the enemy, they could be aliens, they could be anybody, you know. This is about survival. And when he read the script he pointed out that it referred to the Germans seventeen times – he counted them. And he said, 'Doesn't that fight what you're trying to do?' And I thought, yeah, maybe he's right. I'll try removing all of those references. And, I preferred it. It made more sense, you know, using the word 'enemy' instead of using the word 'Germans'. It made it more obvious, in a good way, what we were doing. As in, not showing the Germans, you know?

JONATHAN   Yeah.

CHRISTOPHER   I always talk about letting the audience in on the joke, letting them know that we're not showing the Germans. That's why the Germans are out of focus in the end. You want people to notice, you want them to realize it's deliberate. It's not like, oh, we didn't show much of the Germans. It's we *never* show the Germans, other than the planes.

JONATHAN   And it addresses one of the things that's problematic about war films, starting with *All Quiet on the Western Front,* which is about the First World War – 'the war to end all wars' – because, at the end, it's incredibly nihilistic, right? People could barely remember why it started.

Vietnam-era war movies have a similar level of nihilism to them. World War Two films are problematic because in Western memory there's a sense of it being a virtuous conflict. There was a very recognizable bad guy, they were the worst bad guys, ever. And it tilts the whole narrative in a way. It's interesting that *The Thin Red Line* is set in the Pacific Theater. Certainly the Japanese did terrible things, war atrocities, but there is less of a recognizable, instinctual position of this is good versus evil.

CHRISTOPHER   Right.

JONATHAN   That film is a little more experiential. I know it's one that you and I both love.

CHRISTOPHER   I love it. I think it's one of the best films ever made, maybe the best film ever made. That's how strongly I feel about it. But when I look at it in relation to this, the only relevance it had was a timelessness in the design, and the feel of it. The poetry of it felt totally at odds with Dunkirk and what the story was.

JONATHAN   Sure.

CHRISTOPHER   So it was a question of putting that to one side. I think *The Thin Red Line* in a lot of ways almost feels more like a Vietnam film in the nihilism and the grey areas it's dealing with. There's a different way of looking at the World War Two film issue – which is to say, that if you think of the point of view of somebody passing through those experiences, I don't think the people involved in the situations would have been anywhere near as analytical or as self-reflective as modern movies tend to portray soldiers, tend to portray conflict. I was talking to Matthew McConaughey about this, about a recent film about war, and I asked him what he thought of it and he said, 'Well there's a lot of people having conversations, having a perspective on what they're going through that they would never have had. They would have had later. They wouldn't know what they're going through, you know?' I think that's where the simplicity of World War Two movies lies, even though they can seem jingoistic and too far in the other direction by today's standards. But there is also a truth to that, which is when soldiers go off to war, they can't necessarily think in terms of grey areas. They have to just get on with it. And then, years later, they process the experience.

JONATHAN   One of the details you found which is so interesting to me on the script level, and in the finished film, is that both Tommy and Alex, building on what you're saying, they've gone through this experience. On the one hand, it's a retreat, right?

CHRISTOPHER   Yep.

JONATHAN   But, on the other hand, it's one of the pivotal moments in Western civilization. Certainly, a defeat at Dunkirk, and the rest of the twentieth century would have followed a very, very different contour. Hard to imagine what would have played out with the entire British army trapped in France. An opportunity for the Germans to end the war, essentially. It's a pivotal moment, but one that's almost impossible for the soldiers participating to understand in the moment. Right?

CHRISTOPHER   Yeah.

JONATHAN   One of the things I loved about the script is that unknown quality of what just happened? For Alex and Tommy, when they're asking for the newspaper, Alex is very much in a place where he imagines the public reception for them when they get back home will be very negative, they'll be looked at as cowards. Tommy has a slightly more sanguine take on it based on his reactions. They both misinterpreted their first encounter with civilians when they come back. So they need the newspaper. They need Churchill to tell them what just happened, right?

CHRISTOPHER   Exactly. To tell them what they did and what they went through.

JONATHAN   There are various accounts in which the soldiers during the Second World War were faintly embarrassed by the purple rhetoric coming out, the things that politicians say, contrasted to the experience that they've been having, which was brutal and amorphous and hard to place in that registry. There is something in that moment of needing someone to set the historical moment. Needing a leader to tell you what the fuck just happened.

CHRISTOPHER   I was fascinated by the idea that they wouldn't know what they had done until someone told them. And I think that's an interesting thing you address. Particularly when dealing with Churchill's eloquence. The reason the film ends with the shot of Tommy rather than the shot of the burning plane, because it was scripted ending with the burning plane, which is an apocalyptic image – kind of things to come – but it's a big image. And when I saw the dailies of Fionn reading the Churchill speech and then, at the end, he did this thing where he just, I don't even know what he's doing, but you want to end with this quiet moment with him, where no one's paying attention to him and Alex is eating and drinking stuff the girls are handing through the window. It brings you back to this personal moment: he's trying to process the words he's just read from this very eloquent politician and trying to reconcile that with his experience. Hopefully the audience is trying to do the same thing, through his eyes. So it comes back to a very small thing. I think that is one of the things I was most interested in, because Dunkirk, more than any other, really more than any other historical event that I know of, is a Rorschach test. I've been very interested in talking to Americans over the last two years once I announced what it was I was doing. A disturbing number of people, the first question they would ask me, Are you going to address the fact that Hitler let the British escape? And I was very, very shocked by this.

JONATHAN (*laughter*) Right.

CHRISTOPHER As an English person, first, it's just not something you're particularly aware of as a possibility. And secondly, it simply isn't true. Demonstrably, it's not true. They sank 230 ships. The attempt to destroy the British troops was full on and unambiguous. And there are various reasons why it didn't work, primarily Himmler insisting on doing it with the Luftwaffe because that was the Nazi service that was opposed to the old, aristocratic German army officers. So the Nazis had built the Luftwaffe, and Dunkirk was going to be a demonstration. It was: save the tanks, we'll take care of it. And they weren't able to, for various reasons. I think one of the big reasons is the bombs would drop into the sand and the sand would muffle the explosion, so they were seeing a lot of damage from the air but they weren't actually killing a lot of people. Thankfully. That's the interesting thing about Dunkirk. Even in British culture, it's gone from being a very simple, mythical story of guys in row boats going over, and rowing people across the Channel, which isn't really what happened. It's gone from that and the propaganda stories of the time to, in the eighties, there was a BBC program that gave a very revisionist point of view, where they pointed out, for the first time, that the civilians who went over in the boats were paid for it.

JONATHAN Right. (*Laughter.*)

CHRISTOPHER And, you go, okay, fine, but look into it from today's perspective and you say, well how much were they paid? Expenses?

JONATHAN A nominal thing, but not enough to risk your life.

CHRISTOPHER Absolutely not. There you go, we've missed the wood for the trees. Yes, it was a real human event with flawed and regular people. And there were people who were asked to participate who did not, famously. And there are all kinds of messy things going on. You're talking about hundreds of thousands of people involved. So you can find cowards, you can find heroism. You can find a bit of everything. So the story, the symbol of Dunkirk and the idea of the Dunkirk spirit, becomes a Rorschach test. And when I went with Joshua Levine, our historical advisor, to meet some of the last remaining survivors of the event, one of the questions he asked at least three of them was 'What do you understand about the Dunkirk spirit?' And we got one answer which was, 'It's those little boats coming across and people pulling together.' We got another answer that said, 'It's propaganda, it's bullshit.' Like, it's nothing. Very violently said, I mean, bitterly said. And then someone else saying the Dunkirk spirit was the men holding the perimeter. And that absolutely was his understanding of what the Dunkirk spirit was. Nothing to do with the little ships, nothing to do with that. It was about the guys holding the perimeter, sacrificing themselves to let others escape.

JONATHAN   The men on the line.

CHRISTOPHER   The men on the line – of course, we're not really dealing with that. Because that's a whole other movie. Even the concept of the Dunkirk spirit is understood differently by the people who were involved in it. For the mainstream, it's essentially about people pulling together, it's triumph over terrible odds. But the one guy who was very bitter, just said it was a construct, it was propaganda – I think was the word he used.

JONATHAN   Right, it was a nice speech that Churchill made after the fact.

CHRISTOPHER   This was a guy who didn't want to talk about everything he'd seen, but he'd clearly seen a lot of selfish behavior, a lot of really bad things and felt he'd behaved badly himself, perhaps. But, what you realize when you involve four hundred thousand people in one event, you're going to find everything, you're going to find every aspect. That's what's interesting about it as a story – all those things are true. All the interpretations are valid in a way, and, when we release the film, we'll get all of that noise again. Because there are things that we are saying that people may not agree with. But I feel pretty confident about the broad historical strokes we put in, in terms of the research. It is well researched. It is clear in terms of what the main movements of things are.

JONATHAN   At what point did you decide you wanted to tell the perspective of the expeditionary forces, the soldiers on the beach, and the privateer sailors, the ordinary people coming across to save them, and then, of course, the RAF. Land, air, and sea?

CHRISTOPHER   The process I went through – I've been doing this more and more over the years; I did it with *Interstellar* as well – was just spending months and months just writing notes. You know, not writing anything; I just wouldn't let myself write anything for a very long time. Also, I was waiting for Paramount to do the deal with Warners, and it was an excuse not to write . . . So what I did with *Dunkirk* was I researched, I read first-hand accounts and I got to a point where I understood the scope and movement and the history of what I wanted the film to address, because it's very simple geography. I remember saying to Emma and to Nathan, our production designer – he was on the film already, we got him at a very early stage just to talk about logistics and things. I said I don't want a script. Because I just want to show it, it's almost like I want to just stage it. And film it. And Emma looked at me like I was a bit crazy and was like, okay, that's not really gonna work.

CHRISTOPHER   And I said: okay, fair enough. I did need a script. So, I approached it from a geographical point of view. I knew all the events I wanted to show, and I came up with a structure that let me show that. And I detailed the structure very, very minutely. Figured all of that out before I wrote anything. And then, wrote the script very, very quickly. I mean, weirdly quickly. I just sort of found myself finishing it. It's a very short script, as well – 76 pages.

JONATHAN   Yeah, there's barely any dialogue for the first twenty minutes.

CHRISTOPHER   That's something I really wanted to do. I just wanted to push away from the kind of filmmaking I've been doing where everybody's always explaining things in dialogue.

JONATHAN   (*Laughter.*)

CHRISTOPHER   I just got bored of it . . . no, not bored of it . . .

JONATHAN   It's a professional point of pride here to defend dialogue.

CHRISTOPHER   Absolutely, but I will be coming back to dialogue. No, if I'm to be completely honest, the work I did on *Interstellar*, based on what you had given me, represents for me some kind of peak in terms of how to use dialogue to remind people of things, to make them feel things, to connect things. But I felt like I didn't really have any further to go with that type of filmmaking. I felt genuinely, rightly or wrongly – this is just my subjective feeling – but I felt like I'd kind of mastered that form.

JONATHAN   Sure.

CHRISTOPHER   And done something with it that I was very proud of. It created an emotional story, using the dialogue and all the different bits, the poetry – all these verbal things. Of course, there was a huge visual component to it as well. But you wind up with a three-hour film, almost. With *Dunkirk*, as soon as I talked to people about the fact that I was making that subject, I think they imagined that type of filmmaking, because it's traditionally what you would expect of that subject matter. But that wasn't my interest. What I wanted to do was to go back to the silent films that I love, where they just find a way to use large images and the mass movement of people within the frame to make you feel something, or imagine something. That's why *All Quiet on the Western Front* is a fascinating film because it's got the silent-era mechanics with a little bit of sound. It's right onal phase, and there's a very real sense in which movies for a while – probably for ten or fifteen set them back, because of the technology.

Cinematically, for sure.

PHER Cinematically, you couldn't move the camera. There were great things happening with dialogue, but films became like stage plays for a while. They become very written.

JONATHAN Yeah, a proscenium-style approach.

CHRISTOPHER And, I feel like we have a slightly similar situation with movies now – but reversed. That is to say, movies that are really justifying the big screen. There's a lot of pressure on theatrical windows. And the films that are justifying it right now are the films that are primarily visual. Primarily experiential.

JONATHAN Spectacle.

CHRISTOPHER Spectacle, exactly. And so it's a comfortable area to be working in, with the IMAX format and the big screen and everything. And I'm really trying to push that. When you apply that thinking to this survival story, what I loved about the first-hand accounts that I read is that they're full of, I suppose you'd call it, geographical paradox. I mean the situation itself, on a beach so wide and flat that the big boats can't get in. So you've got these guys queuing up into the water and they can't get to the boats that are out there. Then you have the mole structure out to sea. It's sort of a runway to nothing, a road to nowhere. And there are all kinds of great visual paradoxes, which just seemed very rich for that. Having people talk about who they were, or they've got a girlfriend back home or whatever – I wasn't interested in doing that in this film. I really wanted to explore the Hitchcockian device of shifting allegiances, subjectivity, by virtue of the mechanics of the situation. There's a famous bit in *Psycho*. You have the shower scene with Janet Leigh.

JONATHAN Yeah, and then you switch . . .

CHRISTOPHER   Exactly, your whole emotional investment has been with Janet Leigh and she gets horribly murdered. And then somebody who is complicit in that murder comes in and cleans up the murder scene, puts a body in the trunk of the car, drives the car into the swamp, it starts to sink in the swamp and it stops. And he looks around, 'Oh, am I gonna get caught?' and you're worried he's gonna get caught. And that for me has always been the moment, since somebody pointed it out, I think I was reading a book that analyzed it, that brought it to my attention. I was like, wait, how did that work?

JONATHAN   Yeah, it's a magic trick.

CHRISTOPHER   And the way it works is through the procedure of cleaning it up. The wonderful thing movies can do is visually align you to a character's dilemma in the moment. And I wanted to build a whole script on that, so that it's not about talking about who they were or inspiring sympathy for the characters by virtue of who they were off screen. It's just who are they in that moment, and do I care about them – can they run across that plank? I wouldn't want to have to do that, so I care whether they make it or not. It aims at some sort of idea of pure cinema. It's not that it's superior – I love dialogue in films and I love films that embrace those backstory ideas as well. But I thought it suited a survival story.

The other Hitchcock film I looked at was *Lifeboat*, which is a less successful film, but it's pretty interesting. The whole thing takes place on a lifeboat. You're just there in the moment and with the mechanics of people in that moment. I think that's the fascinating thing about survival – what it does to people. *Treasure of the Sierra Madre*, as well. A favorite of mine. That's a very verbal film, but there's great cinema, there's great geography to it.

JONATHAN   Yeah, and then, at a certain point, your allegiance begins to shift.

CHRISTOPHER   In ways you don't expect.

JONATHAN   So, not much dialogue, but a lot of sound. The sound is very important in this film. And music – when did you start thinking about it? Music is always an important feature of your films. But in this one it feels more so than ever before. You have some very specific, innovative ideas about music in the film. What point did you start thinking about that?

CHRISTOPHER   Well, I started thinking about the relation of the music before I wrote the script.

I settled upon a structure. There's a phenomenon in music called the Shepard Tone that I first explored with Dave Julyan on *The Prestige*. I had basically said to Dave, how do you create a sound for the music that is continually rising in pitch, but never gets anywhere. And he knew of the Shepard Tone phenomenon which is one where by emphasizing different frequencies in the volume of the playing, you do what's called a 'barbershop pole', you have a corkscrew effect. So it always appears to be rising but it never gets out of range. That's an idea that I'm fascinated by. I like optical illusions and I like audio illusions. And so, if you watch *The Dark Knight*, the bat pod that he drives, the engine sound is a Shepard Tone.

It always ascends, it never stalls out, it never gets to the point where you have to reset it. When I wrote the script for *Dunkirk*, I wanted to play with the idea of doing that in the narrative sense, so that you have three different intertwined storylines, and you have them peaking at different moments, so that the idea is that you always feel like you're about to hit – when you're hitting the climax of one episode of the story . . . then another one is halfway through and the other one is just beginning. So there's always a payoff. It's something I've been doing instinctively in the third act sections of my films. *Interstellar* has that in the third act, where you get what's happening on earth crosscutting with what's happening on the ice planet. A lot of that stuff is done in the edit suite, but it's also done at the script stage, where I was naturally trying to produce what I call a snowballing effect, where you're trying to get things to be more than the sum of their parts, so they can get bigger and crazier and bigger and crazier to the point where you think you can't stand it anymore. And the music has always been a huge part of that. The structure of the script is based on the Shepard Tone structure. And so has a rhythmic aspect to it as well, where things are continually feeling faster. They're getting more intense and that's the tricky relationship between the music and the script, which I'm still, still wrestling with.

JONATHAN (*laughter*) In terms of large-format filmmaking – and this is all entirely shot on 65 and 70 mil – was that something you knew, going into it, that you wanted to do?

CHRISTOPHER Our first conversations were that since you've got a big, wide, flat beach, the anamorphic 35 mil aspect ratio might suit it very well. I was talking with Hoyte van Hoytema, my DP, about what's the best way to do this. I'd written a script with very little dialogue. And the thing that had always been holding us back from shooting an entire film in IMAX was the dialogue, because the cameras are loud, so you can't record the dialogue effectively. And with *Interstellar* we'd gotten pretty far, because of the space suits and the microphones on the inside, so we could get more of the dialogue than we'd ever done.

JONATHAN Clean tracks.

CHRISTOPHER And we'd learned that Hoyte could hand hold the IMAX camera and get a spontaneous feel to things. We said, well, there's nothing stopping us at this point, so we should embrace that. We want the film to be spectacular, but we also want it to be experiential. IMAX is the best way to do that. So 70 percent of the film is shot on IMAX, which we've never gone anywhere near before. And then the rest of it is 65 mil 5-perf. So it cuts pretty seamlessly. And the finished prints are going to be all analog, which we've never done before. In the past we've had to digitize and then rerecord sections when we went from IMAX to the 35 mil and vice versa. We're doing these all the old-fashioned way with optical prints. So, they'll have the analog color, they'll have that feeling of an organic kind of film. It should be pretty spectacular.

JONATHAN   Stepping back into your inspiration for this . . . At various moments I try to understand why I wound up working on one project or another – usually with good reasons. But just to track the path of your interest as a filmmaker and how that might have ended different places: do you have a memory or . . . I know that after *Interstellar* you went and visited our grandfather's grave in Amiens, and you knew he'd been in the RAF, as a navigator. Does that connect to this decision?

CHRISTOPHER   I went to see his grave after I went to Dunkirk. The things definitely intertwine, in my mind. We always had a sense of history related to World War Two from Dad. There's always been that strong connection to World War Two because it was so much a part of his life and in losing his father at such a young age.

JONATHAN   He used to be able to tell almost any airplane going overhead.

CHRISTOPHER   That's in the film, yeah. Did you notice that bit?

JONATHAN   Oh, yes, of course. (*Laughter.*)

CHRISTOPHER (*laughter*)   That's Dad. Yeah, it went straight into the film. But, as far as what drew me to this, when I look back on it, yes, that's probably part of it.

JONATHAN   I've taken it for granted that everyone's father can tell whether it's a Merlin engine. (*Laughter.*)

CHRISTOPHER   Exactly. So you watch the film going, yes, of course he knows. He's the dad, right? Most dads can't tell that difference, engines on airplanes. But ours could. And so could Mr Dawson in the film. And, what Dawson shows of Dad is that you feel that he would have quite liked to have flown planes himself, but hasn't for whatever reason. Yes, that aspect – which is why it's nice that Uncle John is in the film and Auntie Kim and our cousins. There's a strong family connection with our Britishness, and what that meant to us growing up. But, if I had to point to an individual element, it was probably Emma and Ivan and myself making the crossing to Dunkirk . . .

JONATHAN   Oh, way back when . . .

CHRISTOPHER   Many years ago, twenty-two years ago, yeah. It was unbelievable. I remember being glad. I had a terrible job at the time, in an office or whatever. And I remember being thrilled to be back at work on Monday after the weekend.

JONATHAN   (*Laughter.*)

CHRISTOPHER   Because it was a very arduous crossing. It took nineteen hours.

JONATHAN   We need some more color there. You guys got stuck in the shipping channels at various moments. Why . . . there was no wind?

CHRISTOPHER   On the way out, there was terrible wind against us, very big seas on the Channel. It was freezing. It was the coldest I've ever been.

JONATHAN   Did you guys go all the way across?

CHRISTOPHER   Yep.

JONATHAN   Pulled in, had a glass of wine, got back on the boat . . .

CHRISTOPHER   Went all the way across, spent a whole day – we were going to go back the next day, but we were like, no, we'll stay an extra day because we were exhausted. So we spent Easter just eating, basically because we hadn't had much food. Because we'd planned for an eight-hour crossing, but it was nineteen hours.

JONATHAN   So you guys went into Dunkirk?

CHRISTOPHER   Yeah. In fact, it's almost that time of year, right now; we were a little earlier in the year, it was Easter time. When I think back on it, it was slightly naive: Oh, well, let's do the crossing to Dunkirk, like they did back then, you know?

JONATHAN   Right.

CHRISTOPHER   And of course it was a very humbling experience because you realize how tough it was. And then, we'd used so much more fuel than we realized, motoring under sail all the way out that we ran out of fuel on the way back and there was no wind and we were stuck in the shipping channel. I mean, it – the whole thing – was mad.

JONATHAN (*laughter*)   How many hours did it take you to come back? Nineteen hours to get there . . .

CHRISTOPHER   I don't remember, but we had to spend the night off Ramsgate because we didn't have any way of getting in to the harbor and everything was closed. It was the bank holiday Monday. All the fuel stores were closed, so Ivan eventually came into Ramsgate under sail, which is a very tricky thing to do and he did it very well, but it was a hairy experience. I remember being so thrilled to be back on dry land. The impression it made on us was indelible because it's something that when you read it in the history books, when you hear it as a story like: 'They got on a little boat and they went over to Dunkirk,' and then you do it and go, no that's a monumental . . .

JONATHAN   It's pretty serious.

CHRISTOPHER   A very serious undertaking. The Channel is not to be trifled with. And that's without people dropping bombs on you! The idea, for example, that you'd get £200 for fuel or that that would motivate you to make that crossing into a war zone – anybody who's ever made that crossing on a small boat, the respect they will have for the people who were involved in these events is massively enhanced, massively.

I think one of the reasons I wanted the film to be very, very intimate is because the things I remember about that crossing are the waves, the way the boat would move, how difficult it was, frankly, to go to the bathroom or something. Just being below decks – just all of that, all the stuff that isn't generally in the history books, but you get from first-hand accounts like the ones that Joshua Levine had put together, which is how I came to know Joshua. But, when you read the first-hand accounts,

xxvi

those are the things that people do remember. It's like how do they go to the bathroom? How do they eat? That's why the film has the bits with them trying to open the tin of pineapples and drink the juice. It's just how do you . . . It begins with a guy looking for a place to go to the bathroom, you know?

JONATHAN   Yeah.

CHRISTOPHER   It's like all the stuff that generally we don't think that much about in those situations. But they are the things we remember. They're the things we would most worry about, simple physical survival. Simple physical comfort. How do you keep doing this? How do you keep going on? You talk to guys who were there who stood in the water for hours at a time, up to their chest in water. For hours and hours. It was interesting when we did all the discussions about how long can the stunt guys be in the water? How long can extras be waist deep in water with wet suits? I was quite worried about the water temperature and then at some point I realized that we were shooting at exactly the time of year that the real evacuation took place. So that answered that question immediately. They did it. And they were getting bombed. So, yeah, they didn't have wet suits. We're gonna have wet suits. We'll be fine, you know?

JONATHAN   In terms of the crossing, the character of George – where did that part of the story come from for you? I think you and I are both sort of allergic to the idea of symbolism in film. I remember reading the script and feeling it's very powerful, very emotional, this story within the film. Where did that come from?

CHRISTOPHER   I had read a couple of different accounts of real people, young people, who went over to Dunkirk. And one of the things that struck me as very sad is the way in which they would be memorialized. Or the way in which they would be portrayed as heroes. In some ways, it made you feel good but, in other ways, it made you feel that there was real pathos, there's a real sense of, you know, what good does it do, somebody whose life's been cut short, to refer to them as a hero? To put them in a newspaper or whatever. For me, that tension is very analogous to the bigger idea of what Dunkirk means.

JONATHAN Yeah, very much.

CHRISTOPHER I wanted some sense of conflict to that. You completely understand it, but you feel conflicted about it. You feel both things at the same time. You feel that somebody in some ways has stepped up and done something great. But then the actual essence of it is pathetic and small and unimportant. And that scale in warfare or in any big geopolitical event is fascinating to me in terms of point of view. The film to me is not about individual heroism; it's about collective heroism. You can have a bunch of people who are acting primarily in their own self-interest and very small in their concerns and really worrying about how to get from A to B. But, overall as a community, there's something that's taking place that's very admirable, and that tension I think is interesting.

JONATHAN George's story gives you a feeling he's an ordinary person but, in getting on the boat in the first place, there's a heroism.

CHRISTOPHER Yeah.

JONATHAN The circumstances of his death are almost banal. Right? And then, seeing his picture in the newspaper makes you feel a little better.

CHRISTOPHER (*laughter*) Yeah, but you also feel worse that you feel better.

JONATHAN I think one of the things I really admire about the film, not to bag on the collective state of English filmmaking right now – but they keep making films about kings and queens, and the landed aristocracy. And one of the things that I really admire about this film is that it connects to our experience, of growing up with a dad who lost his dad in the war, all these people who are remembered individually, they're remembered collectively. This film is about ordinary people. It's not about the generals in tents somewhere, wrestling with noblesse oblige.

CHRISTOPHER   Yeah, and it's not about Churchill. I think it's very important. There's a fascinating thing that happened at the test screenings. We were consistently getting the complaint that people weren't quite sure they'd understood how George dies, or at what moment . . . It's just not enough for people. They completely understand what's happened. They would write on the card: I didn't quite understand that he hit his head on the thing. So, you go: No, you totally get it. It's just not much.

JONATHAN   They're waiting for it to mean something.

CHRISTOPHER   And it doesn't. But that's the whole point. Cillian and I talked extensively when I wanted him to take on the Shivering Soldier role. It wasn't really finished at that point, but I asked him to commit to it. I asked him to trust me; I was like, we'll figure out the resolution of the character together. I said to him, I know how to resolve this character in conventional Hollywood terms. But I don't want to do that. I could give him examples of how we could sort of finish it, but I said that the whole point is there's no right or wrong, it was an accident. There's just shit that happened, basically. So the moment we came up with – ultimately, it became what is one of the most interesting moments of the film, which is where he asks if George is going to be okay and Tom Glynn-Carney, playing Peter, says yeah. He lies to him. I don't think that was even in the script when Cillian signed up for it, so it was a leap of faith on his part. It was like, I'm looking for what's the moment that's in tune with everything that's going on in the film. It's in tune with the perspective of the film, so it's a tiny moment of heroism, I suppose you'd say.

JONATHAN   Right.

CHRISTOPHER   Tiny, tiny, just sparing somebody's feelings. Then I put in the moment where he sees the body anyways.

JONATHAN   Yeah, that's a heartbreaking moment.

CHRISTOPHER   But you've got to be true to the reality of things. If you're going to take a more human tone, you can have the lie to sort of let him off the hook, which I think is a very interesting moment. But then you're gonna to have to follow through – when he got there, wouldn't he see? Wouldn't he know? How's that gonna play out? I think the film, as it's finishing, is very true to all of that – with the notable exception, really, of Farrier, Tom Hardy's character, who is ultimately a bit of a super hero. But, given my fondness for pilots and Spitfire pilots, I don't think it's in me to not do that in the film, if you know what I mean.

JONATHAN   Right.

CHRISTOPHER   On the other hand, he shoots the bomber down and it kills everybody on the ground, so . . .
   Jack Lowden is the other pilot who is looking up at him and when he shoots the bomber you see his eyes light up. It's great, and then he looks down at all the guys and . . .

JONATHAN   He realizes . . .

CHRISTOPHER   The oil, and he's like, oh shit. You always try to allow fate to be arbitrary. That was the challenge for me in the script – and it turned out to be a lot more difficult than I realized to just not allow destiny or fate to be constructed, to be about punishing the bad or rewarding the good. Or ironically punishing the good. It's a very difficult thing to achieve some kind of neutrality, some kind of arbitrary quality to fate. Like trying to create random patterns.

JONATHAN   Yeah.

CHRISTOPHER   I struggled very hard to do it. And then, of course, when you start putting the film together and putting the music on, you're putting the cinematic feeling to it. So everything starts to feel logical, even when it's not supposed to. (*Laughter.*)
   You're fighting the form of movies themselves. We've talked about this for years; it's what I used to call the kind of jump-left thing. You would say to me, well, let's not do that because that's the way movies do it. Yeah, but if you don't do that, if we jump left because everyone usually jumps right . . . you can't just not do it. I always think of it in musical terms. It's like, do we have

to do the crescendo at the end of the song? Well, you kind of do. If you can find a way to do it differently, in an unexpected way, as we did in *The Dark Knight* – you know, with the ferries, which I fought you on for a long time, because I didn't know how to make it work. But you have to have the kinetics. You have to have the thing that makes sense musically or rhythmically. So to try and not reward good people and punish bad people – to try and not push the audience into feeling one way or another about the morality of things – is much harder than I realized. Much harder.

JONATHAN   Especially with the music. Because music can be filled with nuance but it is an extra level of emotional manipulation on the part of the filmmaker, right?

CHRISTOPHER   It is. We've been very objective with the music, so there's very little sentiment in the music.

JONATHAN   Yeah, I noticed that.

CHRISTOPHER   That was a very calculated thing. Even by making something tense or exciting you are manipulating the audience. In a way you are putting a commentary on things, and amplifying things.

JONATHAN   Yeah.

CHRISTOPHER   It's really on the page that you sort these things out. You know, I originally had Gibson burning to death, but when I was getting reactions to the screenplay, it just felt too cruel to a person you like.

JONATHAN   Yeah, I remember feeling that.

CHRISTOPHER   It didn't feel neutral. It felt cruel. It felt like an anti-war statement. And the film is intended to be neutral. I wanted fate to feel arbitrary. And so, in the end, it becomes the Highlander who suffers that fate – which seemed better to me. He's also someone you don't like that much – although the way Brian Vernel played it, I think he's quite relatable, quite engaging. So you get not quite as much of the villainous. Alex is the trickiest version of that – where does he come out? He goes to a pretty unpleasant place, but he's never villainous. What I love about the way Harry Styles played him is that he's very ashamed, he's carrying a lot of weight, and then he sees some pretty girls with pork pies and it's, 'Hey! We're heroes!' You know what I mean?

JONATHAN   (*Laughter.*)

CHRISTOPHER   You know Alex is a simple soul. It's like, actually, what was I worried about? On to the next thing. The way Harry played it feels very real to me.

JONATHAN   It feels right at the center of what the film is doing so much of, which is presenting these events but not telling you how to feel about them. Not pushing you – that's the problem with war films. The problem specifically with World War Two films, which is impossible to unpack. I remember the amazing story about the German houseguest that Mom and Dad had. At one point, Kim came to stay and she was in a revival of *Allo Allo*.

CHRISTOPHER (*laughter*)   I remember that.

JONATHAN   And Dad was in the kitchen and the doorbell rang. And they'd been having this argument with Dad where the German houseguest says the English are obsessed with the Second World War, all the TV programs are about the Second World War. And Dad saying, 'No, it's just a coincidence.' And then the doorbell rings and Dad's in the kitchen and the German houseguest goes to answer the front door, and is greeted by Kim's co-star in full SS uniform. And he says 'Oh, I'm here for Kim.' And the houseguest turns around and here's Aunt Kim coming down the steps in the full Gestapo uniform. (*Laughter.*) Dad had nothing to say. Honestly, the English have made a lot of films about it, more so than other conflicts; it feels like a clear delineation between the good guys and the bad guys. A distinction that isn't really explored in your film at all. I guess this connects to the beginning of our conversation. Did you sort of say, well what's there left to say about the Second World War, what's left to say about war at all beyond *All Quiet on the Western Front*.

And I think in the film you *have* found things that I haven't seen in a war film before. Was that your intention going into it? Was it to try to explore this topic from a perspective you hadn't seen before, or were you more excited about the cinematic possibilities of it?

CHRISTOPHER   Well, I was certainly excited about the cinematic possibilities of it. I think the reason it took a very long time to figure out what kind of film to make was that my initial attraction to it was, and indeed still is, it's just one of the greatest stories ever. And that's really what is always the jumping-off point. There are myriad versions you could make of this story. There's the *Chariots of Fire* version because you've got civilians and the military on parallel courses, kind of interacting. And I struggled for years just trying to figure it out because you're not working in a vacuum. You're working with all this film history. You're working with all of the things that have come before. And having a fresh take on things is important but it's got to be something you're deeply passionate about. One of the reasons it's one of the greatest stories is that it's bizarrely simple. It's biblical in its simplicity. You know how the Bible stories are just four lines – you know, Noah is only a page long.

JONATHAN   (*Laughter.*)

CHRISTOPHER   It's one or two chapters. And the Israelites being driven to the sea by the Egyptians and parting the Red Sea, I don't know how much time it takes up in the Bible, but it's monumental, and I think Dunkirk is like that. You can explain the story to someone in three lines. It's resonant and primal and relatable, and it's never been told . . . in movies. And that's bizarre. There's a 1958 film, but even that one was very much in the tradition of the early post-World War Two films. So the perspective is very different – not just as a sort of isolated story, but in the context of the whole of World War Two, which is the other thing we're doing when I think about it, it's just Dunkirk.

It's not really about the greater World War Two. There's just enough at stake so people know why it was important. I don't think people are going to be waiting for the sequel, if you know what I mean. It's a very self-contained story.

So, as far as bringing something new to it, I felt very strongly that on a mechanical, cinematic level, I could bring something that hadn't been done before – in terms of the structure and the drive, and the simplicity. The film starts with a gunshot and just runs to the end; everything stripped down. And I felt that I had the freedom to do that. Most filmmakers don't have the freedom to do that. So even if they have the idea, even if they have the impetus to do it, getting the freedom to do it on a huge scale is a very difficult thing and I was in a position where I could do that. I could say to the studio, I want to shoot a 76-page script. I want to experiment. The film is very experimental. I wanted to grab that opportunity with one of these great, simple stories. Try that. See what happened.

JONATHAN   Well, let's talk about that non-linear structure just a little bit. Obviously, it's been a hallmark of many films that you've worked on over the years. Here there's a more formal idea from the beginning of taking a week, a day, and an hour and collapsing them into each other. When did that come?

CHRISTOPHER   I think that came from looking at the aerial story. Of wanting to put people in the cockpit of the Spitfire in real time. And when you look at that timescale and you look at how little flying time they had, how much fuel they had, I didn't want to do multiple missions, I wanted to just have that experience in real time. The film is well under two hours, so the proportion of that that's actually in the air is almost literally the real time. I've always been interested in point of view in storytelling. When you look at trying to put the audience very subjectively into the cockpit of the plane, the level of detail that that requires, the concentration on the fuel gage, the charts, the gun sight, the engine and all that, a very limited, small world. In a way, it requires a completely different form of storytelling, because you have to shoot it completely differently; I didn't want to take the camera outside the plane. I really wanted to be true to that. It's about a concentration of detail. It's about the guy wiping his eyes because he's a bit sweaty, and blinking at the sun and looking in the rearview mirror. That has its own timescale, a different timescale to the vast number of people on the beach. There's a sense in which each storyline tries to feel like it's in real time; we try not to do too many time cuts. They have these very different timescales and, mathematically, I wanted to put it together so that they would coincide at a particular point, they'd have a confluence, and then they would separate again. So I did plot it out very carefully. But when you're watching the film, you tend to just experience it. My gamble, in a sense, was that because people are so used to watching war movies where the same sort of thing happens again and again and again, people wouldn't get overly hung up on whether they were understanding the structure or not.

They'd accept the action they're shown, as long as the story's interesting. There's a moment when things come together, where the structure works for people and they start to understand the different timescales. Then they get a bit more enjoyment out of the film, anticipating how it's going to come together. But for me, it was the only way to tell the story because I wanted to cross-cut the Spitfire pilot with a guy who's spending a week on the beach, and I didn't want to do multiple missions and construct extra stories. I wanted to put the audience in that cockpit for the time in which they would engage with a couple of different enemies. So, even the number of planes is quite restrained, but it's a credible mission in terms of the number of encounters and engagements and so forth.

So that pushes you to use the different timescales. And then the boat fits naturally into that because it's one trip back and forth and it's, roughly, a day.

JONATHAN   It speaks to the idea that the human mind takes one tiny perilous moment and expands it.

CHRISTOPHER   Yes.

JONATHAN   And then, for the soldiers on the beach, it's this week-long experience. That is equally extreme and I think cinema can speak uniquely to that.

CHRISTOPHER   It can. It's what I dealt with in *Memento*. It's the scaling of timelines, and cinema is very good at being able to do that. I think of that as a very modern approach, for whatever reason. It's been in literature forever, so it's not modern, but in movies it feels the way we address the modern world. To make you look at it in a different way. And I really wanted to do that with this because I don't want people to be able to look at the subject matter at a remove. People might say, well if you tell a linear story, can't people tap into that better? Well, no – people put it in a box. They look at the uniforms and they put it in a World War Two box. I want them to keep looking at the imagery, to keep feeling like they're in the cockpit, or going, why are we on this tiny boat – all of those things and points of view. I think an aggressively modern storytelling approach wakes that up.

JONATHAN   Yeah.

CHRISTOPHER   And the editing rhythm on this one was different as well. I'm used to just stuffing things tighter and tighter into the box, but this was about letting things breathe. Which, actually, was a follow-on from *Interstellar* because *Interstellar* was a film where, when we tried our usual tricks to tighten the rhythms we looked at the film and it had damaged the movie greatly, because the film had to breathe in certain ways. You had to be able to experience the images – which is one of the reasons I wanted to have a much shorter script for *Dunkirk*. With *Interstellar* it was tricky because there was just no way to get the film away from that three hour mark – I mean 2:49, or whatever it was. It was never going to come down to two and a half hours. It was never going to be a sort of ordinary-size film. But, with this film, it was very important to me that it be lean and stripped down in its story so that the images could breathe a bit. You can experience those things, but still have a manageable size of film.

JONATHAN   In terms of the actual making of a film, it takes two years of often extremely complicated sequences like this film and then you compress it into an hour and 45 minutes. And there's your experience.

CHRISTOPHER   People are always saying, 'How do you get layers into the film? I only spotted this or spotted that,' and I say, I've had years, what do you mean? (*Laughter.*)

JONATHAN   (*Laughter.*)

CHRISTOPHER   You got to sit there and watch it for two hours. If we weren't putting things in there that you couldn't pick up on the first time, we would have failed pretty miserably. In the end, your only job really is to amplify everything, and just make everything as impactful as it can be.

Dunkirk

THE SCREENPLAY

Black screen.

Water slaps hollow metal, metal knocks creaking wood . . .

Super title:

DUNKIRK

Fade in:

Paper. Falling like snow. Six young, filthy Tommys raise their heads along a deserted street, checking rubbish bins, windows . . . One crouches to check a coiled garden hose. He tries the tap – nothing . . .

Title 1:

THE ENEMY HAVE DRIVEN
THE BRITISH AND FRENCH ARMIES TO THE SEA

One Tommy plucks paper from the air . . . Propaganda leaflets showing their position . . . 'YOU ARE SURROUNDED' . . .

Title 2:

TRAPPED AT DUNKIRK,
THEY AWAIT THEIR FATE

He wads the leaflets up, crouches, drops his trousers . . . The Tommy with the hose carefully lifts each side . . .

Title 3:

HOPING FOR DELIVERANCE

He gets a tiny dribble of water which he licks from the nozzle –

Title 4:

FOR A MIRACLE

BLAM BLAM BLAM! Tommy jolts, grabs his trousers. All six race away from us, towards a fence twenty yards away. One by one, five are shot down.The survivor climbs the fence. Gunfire bursts through the fence, ten feet away –

Tommy tries to reload his rifle – fingers struggling with the magazine, training forgotten. Gunfire splinters the fence, five feet away –

Tommy thrusts his index finger into the breech of his rifle again and again, scraping skin. A round jumps into the chamber –

Gunfire three feet away –

Tommy tries once, twice – slides the bolt forward –

Gunfire right next to him –

Tommy spins around, fires blind until empty, scrambles out the back. He races down narrow Dunkirk streets. Breathing. Kit jangling . . . Building after building . . . He rounds a corner –

BLAM! Bullets hit dirt and bricks near him. The street ahead is barricaded, manned by French troops.

TOMMY

ANGLAIS! ANGLAIS!

The French stop firing and wave him through.

He scrambles over their sandbag barricade, taking in their dirty, frightened faces as he passes . . .

A French Soldier grabs him –

FRENCH SOLDIER

Allez, Anglais.

Tommy's mouth opens at the man's bitterness.

FRENCH SOLDIER
(*contempt*)

Bon voyage.

He shoves Tommy down the street behind their protection.

Gunfire behind. Tommy takes off again, hurtling down the dark street, heading towards the blazing light of –

EXT. BEACH AT MALO LES BAINS – CONTINUOUS

The longest, widest beach he's ever seen, sunlight dazzling off the water, endless dark fences snaking across the sand and out into the water. Tommy squints – not fences, lines of men, hundreds of thousands of men . . .

Tommy looks around, clutching his stomach. He clambers over a dune, feverishly undoing his belt, dropping trousers and squatting before he realizes –

He's not alone –

Another soldier, British army shirt undone, sweating with the labour of burying a body. This is Gibson.

The other man notices Tommy, but barely pauses. Tommy finishes, pulls up his trousers and moves towards him. Tommy helps scoop sand over the body.

Tommy notices the corpse's stockinged feet, then watches Gibson stoop to tie his boots . . .

Gibson looks up at him. Tommy shrugs, gestures for Gibson's water can. Gibson hands it over and Tommy takes a swig, carefully catching drops in his hand, then licking them off his palm.

Tommy leaves Gibson buttoning his shirt and heads back onto the beach.

There are destroyers out on the water, too far to reach.

Tommy wanders down to join one of the long, snaking lines which extends into the sea, soldiers up to their chests in water, waiting patiently for ships which do not move.

The man at the back turns to Tommy, unwelcoming. Points at his own insignia.

MAN

Grenadiers, mate.

Tommy moves off. Looks around at other impossibly long lines, At the unattainable ships. Futile.

A line of stretcher-bearers comes past, carrying wounded men along the beach towards the harbour . . .

Looking where they're headed, Tommy sees a long, narrow breakwater extending out into the sea, packed with soldiers. A hospital ship at the end of it.

This breakwater extends a kilometer into the sea. It is called the Mole.

Super title:

1. THE MOLE

one week

Tommy becomes aware of the sound of distant aircraft. Soldiers peer up into the sky . . .

MALE VOICE
(out of shot)

DIVE BOMBERS!

Tommy spots the distinctive kinked wings of the notorious Stuka dive bomber, its nightmarish howl rising as it picks up speed, diving at the beach . . .

The lines of men instantly vanish – soldiers scattering back to the dunes, burrowing into the sand . . . The first bombs lift sand into the air.

The stretcher-bearers put down their loads, lying across them, protecting them as the area is hammered . . .

The first Stuka pulls out of its dive, revealing two more Stukas diving. There are nine more about to follow . . .

Tommy sees a soldier lying on his back, rifle aimed at the sky, firing defiantly, desperately at the attacking plane . . . The ground around him lifts into the air with the second wave of bombs.

Tommy buries his face in the sand as the bombs blast and blast and blast –

The explosions stop. Tommy lifts his head. BOOM! Another wave of bombs explodes in series up the beach. Then, finally, quiet. Tommy rises . . .

The stretcher-bearers, back on their feet, lift their burdens (four bearers per stretcher, one at each corner).

Several stretchers are left behind on the sand.

Soldiers on the beach watch in despair as one of the destroyers is slipping below the water, smoke billowing.

MALE VOICE

WHERE'S THE BLOODY AIR FORCE?!

Cut to:

EXT. ENGLISH COAST, WEYMOUTH HARBOUR – MORNING

A lanky youth runs down to the masts of the crowded harbour.

He races along the wooden dock, jumping over ropes as he rushes to a large yacht, the Moonstone.

Super title:

2. THE SEA

one day

The youth, George (seventeen), leaps from the dock into the well. Two naval officers emerge from the cabin, pushing past. George watches them go, confused . . .

Mr Dawson (fifties, civilian dress) hands George a stack of china plates and ducks back inside.

A second young man, Peter (nineteen), emerges, carrying boxes.

> PETER
> Navy's requisitioned her – there's some men across the Channel, at Dunkirk, need taking off. (*Points at dock.*) They told us to strip her and load those life jackets.

George looks along at the dock. At a pile of hundreds of life jackets. George looks at Peter. Surprised.

> GEORGE
> *Some* men?

> PETER
> Navy'll be back in an hour. My dad wants to be ready before then . . .

Cut to:

EXT. SKY – DAY

Moving through billowy peaks, three sleek, beautiful Spitfires streak into frame. Elegant. In confident formation.

Super title:

3. THE AIR

one hour

INT. COCKPIT, SPITFIRE 1 — CONTINUOUS

The pilot, Farrier, has a light touch on the controls. He checks his left and right, scanning the skies.

> VOICE ON RADIO
> Check fuel, Fortis 1 and 2.

Farrier reaches forward to his fuel gauge, pushes the button beside it – the needle shoots up to three-quarters full.

> FARRIER
> Seventy gallons.

INT. COCKPIT, SPITFIRE 2 — CONTINUOUS

The pilot, Collins, checks his fuel gauge –

> COLLINS
> Sixty-eight gallons, Fortis Leader.

> FORTIS LEADER
> (*over radio*)
> Stay down at five hundred feet to leave fuel for forty minutes fighting time over Dunkirk.

> COLLINS
> Understood. Vector 128, angels point five.

INT. COCKPIT, SPITFIRE 1 — CONTINUOUS

Farrier checks his chart.

> FORTIS LEADER
> Keep an eye on that gauge, even when it gets lively – save enough to get back.

With a glance at his fuel gauge, Farrier pulls on the stick.

EXT. SKY – CONTINUOUS

The three planes bank left in perfect harmony as we –

Cut to:

EXT. BEACH AT LA PANNE – LATE AFTERNOON

Tommy looks down at several patients on stretchers left behind, bearers dead or disappeared . . .

One of them groans. Still alive.

Tommy looks around. Gibson is there.

They grab the stretcher and hustle down the beach towards the mole . . .

EXT. BASE OF THE MOLE – CONTINUOUS

A Warrant Officer tries to keep order as men line up to start the shuffle out along the eight-foot wide concrete mole.

The line of stretcher-bearers approaches . . .

From the base all you can see is the the backs of helmeted heads queuing out onto the narrow breakwater.

The Warrant Officer sees the stretchers, waves them past –

> WARRANT OFFICER
> Along the mole. All the way, she's leaving –

A ships's whistle –

> WARRANT OFFICER
> That's it. (*He turns.*) MAKE WAY! MAKE WAY!

The stretcher-bearers squeeze past . . .

EXT. BEACH – CONTINUOUS

Tommy and Gibson hear the ship's whistle. They start running with the stretcher, heading for the base of the mole . . .

EXT. BASE OF THE MOLE – CONTINUOUS

The Warrant Officer addresses a group of French soldiers.

> WARRANT OFFICER
> NO FRENCH! NON FRANÇAISES – SEULEMENT ANGLAISES! ENGLISH ONLY, YOU'LL HAVE YOUR OWN SHIPS!

Tommy and Gibson arrive, panting. The Warrant Officer looks at them. The ship's whistle – the Warrant Officer points up –

> WARRANT OFFICER
> That's two minutes – you've missed it.

He turns back to arguing with the French . . .

Tommy pushes forward with the stretcher. Soldiers try to let him through on the narrow mole –

The Warrant Officer, seeing Tommy, just shakes his head.

EXT. HOSPITAL SHIP – CONTINUOUS

Stretchers are loaded up the gangplank onto the deck of the ship, supervised by a Petty Officer.

He checks his watch, then looks along the mole at the remaining stretchers . . .

EXT. THE MOLE – CONTINUOUS

Tommy weaves along the mole, squeezing past the mass of troops jamming the breakwater . . .

Tommy leans out over the edge where the rail is missing, a twenty-foot drop to the churning water . . .

Gibson follows, echoing Tommy's route and footing.

EXT. HOSPITAL SHIP – CONTINUOUS

The last of the line of stretchers is carefully, awkwardly raised up from the mole onto the deck of the ship. The Petty Officer speaks urgently to the last stretcher-bearer.

PETTY OFFICER

Last?

The Stretcher-Bearer nods, too breathless to speak, then follows his colleagues back down off the ship.

An explosion hits the water nearby –

Everyone hits the deck as shells impact the water.

EXT. THE MOLE – CONTINUOUS

Tommy is pulled up short as Gibson stumbles –

An ME 109 strafes the length of the mole with gunfire – soldiers hit the deck, several are hit . . .

Gibson struggles up.

Cut to:

EXT. WEYMOUTH HARBOUR – DAY

Peter and George rush things off the boat, then start loading the orange life-preservers. Mr Dawson looks up from his charts to see naval officers and crew coming along the harbour, assigning crew members to boats . . .

Peter follows his gaze –

INT. MOONSTONE – CONTINUOUS

Peter bursts into the cabin, stacking life vests.

EXT. MOONSTONE – CONTINUOUS

The pile of life vests on the dock shrinks . . . Mr Dawson watches the naval men coming closer –

Cut to:

INT. COCKPIT, SPITFIRE 1 – CONTINUOUS

Farrier lightly brushes his fingers over the dashboard.

> COLLINS
> (*over radio*)
> Dunkirk's so far, why can't they load at Calais?

Farrier looks over at his wing mate, Collins (Fortis 2).

> FORTIS LEADER
> (*over radio*)
> The enemy had something to say about it.

INT. COCKPIT, SPITFIRE 2 – CONTINUOUS

Collins scans the skies above . . .

> COLLINS
> Down here we're sitting ducks.

> FORTIS LEADER
> (*over radio*)
> Keep 'em peeled. They'll come out of the sun.

INT. COCKPIT, SPITFIRE 1 – CONTINUOUS

Farrier looks around into the blinding sun . . .

Cut to:

EXT. HOSPITAL SHIP – CONTINUOUS

The Petty Officer barks orders at the crew –

> PETTY OFFICER
> Man the bow line! Ready on the stern!

Troops stuck down on the mole below look resentfully at the ship preparing to depart. One Soldier calls up –

> SOLDIER
> Any more room?

The Petty Officer glares down at him.

EXT. THE MOLE – CONTINUOUS

Tommy breaks through a tight crowd of soldiers and stops.

In front of him is a jagged chasm. One narrow plank laid across it. The drop is fifteen feet to rocks and concrete below.

The ship's whistle sounds. Tommy stares –

> SOLDIER
> Take a run at it!

Tommy glances at the Soldier who spoke. Looks back at Gibson.

> TOMMY
> One, two, three!

Tommy bolts across, pure concentration, the plank bowing and bouncing as he crosses the middle, Gibson following. Tommy's foot slips, he almost goes over, rights himself –

Helpful arms grab them as they hit the other side, a couple of cheers from the crowd. Tommy ploughs on –

EXT. HOSPITAL SHIP – CONTINUOUS

Tommy passes the stretcher-bearers coming back down the

mole. One of them moves to help but Tommy shakes his head, pushing past . . .

The Petty Officer gestures at his men to pull the gangplanks –

> PETTY OFFICER
> PULL THE GANGPLANKS!

Tommy and Gibson arrive at the end of the mole.

> TOMMY
> Oi!

A gangplank is shoved back down.

They struggle up it with the stretcher.

When they make it to the deck they practically drop their burden, gasping for breath. Orderlies takes the stretcher below.

Tommy and Gibson look around for a place to perch, catching their breaths . . .

Cut to:

EXT. MOONSTONE – CONTINUOUS

Mr Dawson sees the Naval Officers stepping onto their dock –

> MR DAWSON
> Ready on the stern line.

George hops onto the dock, unties the stern line. Stops. Looks at the approaching Officers. Then back to Mr Dawson –

> GEORGE
> Aren't you waiting for the navy?

Mr Dawson starts the engine. Peter jumps down onto the boat with the bow rope . . .

> MR DAWSON
> They've asked for the *Moonstone*, they'll have her. With her captain.

PETER

And his son.

The boat moves off. Peter looks to catch the line from George.

PETER

Thanks for the help, George.

Who, instead, jumps onto the stern, to Peter's surprise.

PETER

You know where we're going?

GEORGE

France.

MR DAWSON

Into war, George.

GEORGE

I'll be useful, sir.

Mr Dawson looks at George. Pushes the throttle forward and they motor out of the harbour into the English Channel . . .

Cut to:

INT. COCKPIT, SPITFIRE 2 – DAY

Collins spots something –

INT. COCKPIT, SPITFIRE 1 – DAY

Farrier spots the ME 109 coming out of the sun –

FARRIER

Bandit – eight o'clock.

FORTIS LEADER
(*over radio*)

Break.

EXT. SKY OVER ENGLISH CHANNEL – CONTINUOUS

The three Spitfires dart away from each other. The German plane takes the left one (Collins), hurtling down –

INT. COCKPIT, SPITFIRE 2 – CONTINUOUS

Collins dives, rolling, glancing back –

> COLLINS
>
> He's on me!

INT. COCKPIT, SPITFIRE 1 – CONTINUOUS

Farrier banks around, lining up on Collins' pursuer.

> FARRIER
>
> And I'm on him –

Cut to:

EXT. HOSPITAL SHIP – EVENING

Tommy and Gibson shuffle around the deck, looking for a spot to settle . . .

The Able Seaman manning the gangplank calls over –

> ABLE SEAMEN
>
> You two, get a shift on!

Tommy reluctantly follows Gibson onto the plank.

EXT. THE MOLE – CONTINUOUS

As he shuffles down the gangplank he looks over at the thousands queuing on the mole . . .

A Second Lieutenant on the mole waves Tommy along –

> SECOND LIEUTENANT
>
> Off you go! Back up the line!

As Tommy steps off the plank he hears a noise: Gibson, finger to his lips, 'shush', is crouched in the crisscross structure below the mole where he can't be seen by the officers on top. He beckons Tommy to join him . . .

PETTY OFFICER
That last barrage damaged the rudder!

The Second Lieutenant turns to the Petty Officer. Tommy slips down beside Gibson –

SECOND LIEUTENANT
Tie up again while we try to fix it.

They settle in on the beams just above the water line . . .

Cut to:

EXT. MOONSTONE, ENGLISH CHANNEL – MORNING

Mr Dawson comes to the back of the well, fits the tiller, to steer from outside, Peter at his side. George, on the bow, looks across at several naval vessels on the same course.

Suddenly he spots a bomber overhead –

GEORGE
Mr Dawson!

Mr Dawson's eyes don't leave his course –

MR DAWSON
One of ours, George.

George looks up as the plane. A Blenheim bomber passes over.

Looking down to his left – a fishing trawler bobbing along. Further back down the convoy his sees a Thames paddle steamer.

A destroyer approaches from the opposite direction. As George peers, he starts to make out shapes of men on the decks.

The destroyer passes close enough that George can see the boat is packed with soldiers. Weary, bedraggled, dispirited soldiers. George stares at the haunted faces.

As the Moonstone rides over the wake of the destroyer, an ominous boom reverberates in the distance. Too sudden for thunder, the boom multiplies into a distant barrage . . .

Mr Dawson comes forward, drawn by the sound. He stares at the horizon – distant black smoke precisely where they're headed. More booms. Mr Dawson looks at George. Who is scared. He puts his hand on his shoulder. Nods reassuringly.

Cut to:

INT. COCKPIT, SPITFIRE 1 – CONTINUOUS

Farrier concentrates, trying to angle his plane at the tail of the ME 109 ahead . . . but the German plane keeps pulling out of his sights, turning right, pulling g's, rolling . . .

FARRIER
On my mark – draw him left, Fortis 2 . . . Three, two, one, mark –

INT. COCKPIT, SPITFIRE 2 – CONTINUOUS

Collins pulls hard left, rolling up and left as tracer fire streaks past.

INT. COCKPIT, SPITFIRE 1 – CONTINUOUS

Farrier watches the ME 109 cut left to follow Collins. He pushes the button on his stick to strafe the plane with his cannons . . . Smoke starts trailing from the German plane.

FARRIER
Clear.

EXT. SKY OVER ENGLISH CHANNEL – CONTINUOUS

The ME 109 trails heavy smoke as it tips towards the water–

INT. COCKPIT, SPITFIRE 2 – CONTINUOUS

Collins straightens out, tries to look back –

COLLINS

Is he down?

INT. COCKPIT, SPITFIRE 1 – CONTINUOUS

Farrier watches the ME 109 smash into the water, breaking up in a fiery mess –

FARRIER

Down for the count –

Tracer fire smashes into Farrier's plane, sparking inside and out. Farrier banks hard right as a second 109 streaks away. He straightens up.

FARRIER

Fortis leader, one bandit down . . .

Nothing.

Fortis Leader, do you read?

Nothing.

Farrier looks around, spots a Spitfire –

FARRIER

Fortis 2, I have you to port – no eyes on Fortis Leader. Over.

COLLINS
(over radio)

Understood, Fortis 1. Orbit for a look . . .

Farrier looks all around as he pulls right on the stick . . .

Cut to:

EXT. THE MOLE – EVENING

Eerie quiet.

Tommy and Gibson sit in the structure, unseen, listening . . .

Commander Bolton checks progress on board the hospital ship.

>   COMMANDER BOLTON
> How long, Lieutenant?

>   LIEUTENANT
> We need to run a new cable, sir. They're scrambling.

Commander Bolton turns to Colonel Winnant, the army representative.

>   COMMANDER BOLTON
> Colonel, you're going to have to decide how many more
> wounded to evacuate . . . one stretcher takes the space of
> seven standing men.

Colonel Winnant takes this in.

Tommy crouches lower as he sees a launch approach . . .

A high-ranking officer is helped up the ladder onto the mole.

>   COMMANDER BOLTON
>   (*salutes*)
> Rear Admiral.

>   REAR ADMIRAL
> Commander. (*To Colonel Winnant.*) At ease, Colonel.
> How's the perimeter?

Colonel Winnant gestures towards the smoke-shrouded town –

>   COLONEL WINNANT
> Shrinking every day. But between our rearguard and the
> French . . . we're holding the line. And the enemy tanks've
> stopped.

COMMANDER BOLTON
Why?

COLONEL WINNANT
Waste precious tanks, when you can pick us off from the
air, like fish in a barrel?

COMMANDER BOLTON
How long does London expect the army to hold out before
we make terms?

The Rear Admiral looks sharply at the idea.

REAR ADMIRAL
Make terms? They're not stopping here. We need to get
our army back.

The Rear Admiral points across the dark water . . .

Britain's next. Then the world.

Commander Bolton puts his field glasses to his face.

COMMANDER BOLTON
Christ, you can almost see it from here. . .

COLONEL WINNANT
What?

COMMANDER BOLTON
Home. (*Turns to the town.*) What about the French?

REAR ADMIRAL
Publicly, Churchill's told them *bras dessous.* (*Off look.*)
Arm in arm. Leaving together.

COLONEL WINNANT
And privately?

REAR ADMIRAL
We need our army back.

COLONEL WINNANT
How many men are they talking about?

REAR ADMIRAL
Churchill wants thirty thousand. Ramsay's hoping we can give him forty-five.

Commander Bolton looks out at the mass of humanity.

COMMANDER BOLTON
There are four hundred thousand men on this beach, sir.

Down below, Tommy takes this in. Every man for himself.

REAR ADMIRAL
We'll just have to do our best.

Bolton straightens up.

COMMANDER BOLTON
Right, this mole stays open at all costs.

Bolton points at the funnel and masts of sunken ships.

We're in range of artillery from the west – anything else sinks out here, the mole's blocked and we're stuffed.

REAR ADMIRAL
Can't we load from the beaches?

COLONEL WINNANT
Better than standing out here when the dive bombers come.

COMMANDER BOLTON
Impossible.

The Rear Admiral looks at the lines of men on the beaches.

REAR ADMIRAL
Too shallow.

COMMANDER BOLTON
Anything drafting more than three feet can't get near. We don't have enough small boats to ferry men out to the destroyers.

The Rear Admiral nods.

The mole it is, then, gentlemen.

Cut to:

EXT. MOONSTONE, ENGLISH CHANNEL — DAY

Mr Dawson is on the bow, peering ahead. The distant smoke is closer, small shapes in the sky move above distant ships, accompanied by thunderous booms . . .

Much nearer: a shape. A wreck. Upside down.

Mr Dawson moves quickly down the yacht to the well and takes the helm, throttling back. He gestures for Peter to head to the bow.

The Moonstone *approaches the wreck. Bodies surround the overturned hull.*

Crouched on the hull – a Soldier.

Mr Dawson reverses the screw, slowing to a crawl. Peter stares out at the Shivering Soldier.

PETER
Can you swim it?

The Shivering Soldier stares back at Peter. Peter looks back at Mr Dawson.

Can you get closer?

Mr Dawson looks down the side of the boat, considers.

MR DAWSON
Can't risk it!

Mr Dawson turns to George.

Take Peter a line.

George grabs a coiled rope and heads up to the bow. Peter takes the rope from George –

PETER

I'll throw you a line!

The Shivering Soldier looks up at him, blank. Peter tosses the line. It hits the water several feet in front of the soldier who stares at it.

Peter gathers the line, then tosses it again.

The Shivering Soldier springs for it, grabbing it and hanging on as Peter and George reel him in, pulling him around to the stern ladder.

He is too exhausted to make it up the ladder, so they grab his shirt, pulling him into the well.

George grabs a blanket and puts it around the Soldier's shoulders.

Mr Dawson glances at the Soldier, then reverses from the wreck the way he came in, and steers wide around the visible portion of the wreck.

Once the water ahead is open, Mr Dawson speeds up, heading again for the dark smoke of Dunkirk.

Cut to:

EXT. SKY ABOVE THE ENGLISH CHANNEL – DAY

The two Spitfires arc around the wreckage of the ME 109 . . .

INT. COCKPIT, SPITFIRE I – CONTINUOUS

Farrier spots something –

FARRIER

Wreckage below.

He heads low over the wreckage.

COLLINS
(*over radio*)
More of the 109?

Farrier banks, looking down, spots a half submerged tail –
clearly RAF.

FARRIER
No, it's Fortis Leader, over.

COLLINS
Do you think he got out?

FARRIER
Didn't see a 'chute.

Farrier straightens up. Considers.

FARRIER
Record his position, then set heading 128, height . . . one
thousand, over.

COLLINS
Vector 128, angels 1. Understood.

Farrier reaches forward, pushes the button by his fuel gauge . . .
Nothing.

The glass is cracked. He taps it with his glove. Nothing.

FARRIER
Fortis 2, what's your fuel?

INT. COCKPIT, SPITFIRE 2 – CONTINUOUS

Collins checks his gauge.

COLLINS
Fifty gallons, over.

INT. COCKPIT, SPITFIRE I — CONTINUOUS

Farrier takes this down with a grease pencil . . .

> FARRIER
>
> Keep letting me know – my gauge took a knock back
> there, over.

> COLLINS
>
> Should you turn back?

Farrier methodically checks his other gauges and switches . . .
checks the responsiveness of rudder, ailerons . . .

> FARRIER
>
> I'm confident it's just the gauge.

Farrier glances at his pencil mark, sets the bezel on his watch.

He taps his gauge one more time. Nothing.

Cut to:

EXT. THE MOLE — EVENING

Bolton watches the Rear Admiral motor away in his launch, the
engine noise fading to be replaced by –

A familiar, dreaded sound, building. Stukas.

The men on the mole look up at the sky.

From high above we see how trapped and exposed this line of
men stretching a kilometer into the sea really is.

Restless, the soldiers look behind and in front. There's simply
nowhere to go. The awful whine builds. Then changes pitch as
the bombers go into their dive.

BOOM BOOM BOOM BOOM BOOM! The bombs impact
the sea either side of the mole. Soldiers crouch as low as they
can –

The onslaught is endless, terrible and inescapable.

BOOM! A direct hit to the hospital ship –

The Stukas have gone.

Screams and shouts – people start jumping over the side of the hospital ship onto the mole . . .

VOICES

She's going down! SHE'S GOING UNDER!

Commander Bolton shouts at the men manning the lines.

COMMANDER BOLTON

CUT HER LOOSE!

The crew are jumping off the side, the burning ship is sinking.

SUB-LIEUTENANT

What about the wounded?

COMMANDER BOLTON

Cut her loose, and push her off! We can't let her sink at the mole!

The men cast her off and push her off. Crew members and orderlies leap from the deck into the water –

The bow of the blazing, sinking ship drifts away from the mole.

Tommy and Gibson pull soldiers up onto the beams of the mole.

As the bow comes around, the stern scrapes along the wooden pilings, splintering them in its path –

A flailing soldier is in its path, trying to swim free –

The steel hulk is about to crush him –

Tommy grabs him by the shoulders and yanks with all his might, pulling him clear just as the hull grinds against the wood. Tommy looks down on the breathless, wet soldier. The wet soldier focuses on Tommy.

This is Alex. He nods thanks. Tommy nods back.

Commander Bolton watches the ship slip down into the waves.

Cut to:

EXT. MOONSTONE, ENGLISH CHANNEL – DAY

Mr Dawson is back at the helm. The Shivering Soldier sits in the well, blanket over his shoulders. Staring at the deck. George watches him, then leans forward.

>   GEORGE
> Come below – it's out of the wind.

The Shivering Soldier glances at the companionway. Shakes his head.

>   GEORGE
> Really – it's warmer.

George reaches out for the Shivering Soldier's arm – who smacks it away –

>   MR DAWSON
> Leave him, George.

George looks up at the Commander.

>   MR DAWSON
> He feels safer on deck. You would too if you'd been
> bombed –

>   SHIVERING SOLDIER
> U-boat. It was a U-boat.

>   PETER
> Get him some tea, George.

George darts downstairs. Useful.

Cut to:

EXT. SKY OVER ENGLISH CHANNEL – DAY

The two Spitfires head towards the massive black smoke hanging over the distant port of Dunkirk.

There are many different ships and boats of all sizes in the water in front of them . . .

INT. COCKPIT, SPITFIRE 2 – CONTINUOUS

Collins pushes the button to check the fuel gauge –

> COLLINS
> Forty gallons, Fortis 1, over.

INT. COCKPIT, SPITFIRE 1 – CONTINUOUS

Farrier instinctively looks at his gauge. Nothing.

> FARRIER
> Forty gallons, understood.

Farrier pulls out a grease pencil and notes fuel and time.

> We're about five minutes out – climb to two thousand.

> COLLINS
> (*over radio*)
> That's more fuel.

> FARRIER
> I don't want to get jumped again. Get some altitude, dive down on the bastards. Over.

> COLLINS
> (*over radio*)
> Understood. Angels two, over.

Farrier pulls back on the stick –

EXT. SKY OVER ENGLISH CHANNEL — CONTINUOUS

The Spitfires rise gloriously into higher air . . .

Cut to:

EXT. THE MOLE — EVENING

Commander Bolton looks over at the wet soldiers clinging to the understructure of the mole.

> COMMANDER BOLTON
> (*out of shot*)
> Right, Highlanders. Let's find you another ship.

The wet soldiers pull themselves to their feet . . .

Tommy, watched by Alex, slips into the water, then pulls himself out, dripping. Gibson follows suit. Alex laughs at them . . . then helps them push into the group.

They follow the wet soldiers up onto the mole, where Bolton's men shepherd them onto a launch.

EXT. LAUNCH — CONTINUOUS

Tommy and Gibson make themselves inconspicuous among the Highlanders, eyes down.

As the launch pulls away from the mole, Tommy glances back at the men lining the breakwater.

The launch motors out of the harbour.

It approaches a destroyer, its sheer iron side towering above the launch, as it bobs up and down alongside.

Cargo nets are dropped over the side, and the men start to step up onto the rail of the bobbing ship, waiting for the rhythmic movement towards the iron wall, grabbing at the rope mesh, struggling to pull themselves up.

Tommy steps up to the railing, next to an exhausted soldier who can barely lift himself up. Tommy grabs his shoulder to steady him on the rail as the launch bounces off the iron wall of the destroyer.

They both grab at the net, Tommy climbing up –

The exhausted soldier has not got his feet into the netting, he slips lower . . .

The gap between the launch and the destroyer shrinks to nothing –

The soldier's legs are crushed between the two oblivious craft-He screams – hands pull him up as the craft separate . . .

EXT. DESTROYER – CONTINUOUS

The men collapse onto the deck in exhausted piles. Sailors and Nurses urge them to move below decks.

SAILOR

Down below. Come on, mate –

Tommy follows Alex and his mates to a doorway at the head of the stairs down below. A Nurse is standing there.

NURSE

Come on, boys. There's a nice cup of tea for you down there. This way, come on.

INT. DESTROYER – CONTINUOUS

Tommy starts down the stairs. Gibson has stopped at the top, looking down into the stairwell.

NURSE

Come on, down you go –

Gibson, shaking his head, steps back.

Alex sees this – turns to follow Tommy into the crowd in the hold. They are handed a cup of tea each and a hunk of bread.

EXT. DESTROYER – CONTINUOUS

Out on deck, Gibson sits by the companionway in the gathering dark as the ship gets under way . . .

INT. HOLD, DESTROYER – CONTINUOUS

Down below, Tommy and Alex eat and drink hungrily and gratefully. Between bites, Alex gestures to the stairs.

ALEX
What's wrong with your friend?

Tommy watches the door to the hold close. Takes another bite. Uneasy.

Looks around the hold, packed like the tube at rush hour.

TOMMY
Looking for a quick way out. In case we go down.

Tommy and Alex edge through the crowd towards the stairs . . .

Cut to:

EXT. MOONSTONE, ENGLISH CHANNEL – DAY

George hands the Shivering Soldier a steaming mug of tea.

The BOOMS start reverberating again.

The Shivering Soldier glances up. Realizes something . . .

SHIVERING SOLDIER
Where are we going?

MR DAWSON
Dunkirk.

SHIVERING SOLDIER
No, we're going to England!

MR DAWSON
We have to go to Dunkirk first.

                    SHIVERING SOLDIER
     I'M NOT GOING BACK!

*Peter watches from the companionway. The Shivering Soldier
throws his arm out at the dark cloud on the horizon –*

                    SHIVERING SOLDIER
     Look at it! We go there we'll die!

Mr Dawson looks at the Shivering Soldier. Calm.

                    MR DAWSON
     I see your point, son. Take your tea below and warm up
     while we plot a course.

*The Shivering Soldier considers this. Then takes his blanket and
heads down the companionway. Peter helps him down below.*

INT. CABIN, MOONSTONE – CONTINUOUS

*Peter opens the door to the forepeak and sits the Shivering
Soldier down on a narrow bunk.*

                    PETER
     I'll get you some more tea.

Peter shuts the door. Looks at the bolt. Considering.

EXT. MOONSTONE – CONTINUOUS

*George looks up at the Commander. Addresses him with the
tone of a child trying to speak like a grown-up . . .*

                    GEORGE
     Is he a coward?

Mr Dawson looks sharply at George.

                    MR DAWSON
     He's shell-shocked, George. He's not himself. He may
     never be himself again.

                          34

INT. CABIN, MOONSTONE — MOMENTS LATER

Peter hands the Shivering Soldier a cup of tea. The Shivering Soldier accepts it wordlessly. Staring in front of him. Peter closes the forepeak door. Pauses.

Peter gently slides the bolt.

Cut to:

INT. COCKPIT, SPITFIRE 1 — DAY

Farrier looks down at the mass of ships and boats passing each other. There is the minesweeper, Castor, every inch of her deck covered with troops —

> COLLINS
> (*over radio*)
> Heinkel, eleven o'clock, lining up to drop her load on that minesweeper —

Farrier's head snaps around — spots the German bomber —

> FARRIER
> Fighters?

INT. COCKPIT, SPITFIRE 2 — CONTINUOUS

Collins peers down, scanning around the Heinkel bomber for its fighter escort . . . Spots —

> COLLINS
> 109s — off her starboard —

> FARRIER
> (*over radio*)
> I'm on the bomber.

Collins pushes forward into a dive . . .

EXT. SKY OVER ENGLISH CHANNEL — CONTINUOUS

Spitfire 2 dives at the German fighters, cannons blasting . . .

Spitfire 1 dives at the German bomber, cannons blasting . . .

INT. COCKPIT, SPITFIRE 1 — CONTINUOUS

Farrier has the Heinkel in his sights, bucking and weaving as his Spitfire slices down through turbulent air . . . He pushes the button on the stick which controls his guns . . .

He rolls away from the Heinkel as he dives beneath it, taking his finger off the trigger, fighting the g's with his neck as he pulls out of the dive . . .

INT. COCKPIT, SPITFIRE 2 — CONTINUOUS

Collins fires at one of the 109s until he sees smoke trailing. He dives between the German planes . . .

INT. COCKPIT, SPITFIRE 1 — CONTINUOUS

Farrier scans his surroundings as he tries to orient himself relative to the Heinkel . . .

Finding it, he pulls the stick, lining up for another run at it, this time from below . . .

The bomber is in his sights – he fires his guns . . .

He flashes past, dangerously close to its top turret which hurls tracer bullets at him. He sees sparking on the hull of the bomber –

INT. COCKPIT, SPITFIRE 2 — CONTINUOUS

Coming around, starting to climb, Collins sees the Heinkel veer off course, heading away from the minesweeper –

                    COLLINS
She's turning – you must've damaged her.

                    FARRIER
                  (*over radio*)
Where's the escort?

                    COLLINS
I got one of –

*BLAM BLAM BLAM!! Cannon fire rips into Spitfire 2. Collins
yanks the stick but it's too late. Flames leap from the fuselage . . .*

                    COLLINS
I'm going down.

                    FARRIER
                  (*over radio*)
I'm on him – bail out.

*Collins checks his parachute, opens the canopy. The wind howls
inside the cockpit. He surveys the water below – slides his
canopy shut again.*

                    COLLINS
The swell looks good, I'm ditching.

Cut to:

INT. HOLD, DESTROYER – NIGHT

The munching and slurping of starving soldiers.

The engines kick into gear as the destroyer starts to move –

A cheer goes up around the hundreds of men in the hold . . .

EXT. DESTROYER – CONTINUOUS

*Up on deck, Gibson watches several row boats heading towards
them. Hearing the engines, they start shouting –*

37

MALE VOICES

Wait! Wait for us!

Gibson spots white water on the black sea – a wake –

MALE VOICE
(*out of shot*)

TORPEDO!

An explosion lifts water at the side of the ship –

INT. HOLD, DESTROYER – CONTINUOUS

The cheering stops, Boooooms shudder the suddenly fragile iron walls of the hold, massive percussions of wobbling metal sheets.

EXT. DESTROYER – CONTINUOUS

A blast that moves every bolt of the destroyer –

INT. HOLD, DESTROYER – CONTINUOUS

Anyone standing is thrown off their feet –

EXT. DESTROYER – CONTINUOUS

A vast plume of fire explodes up and out of the funnel. The deck blasts apart –

INT. HOLD, DESTROYER – CONTINUOUS

Men scream as the iron plates of the walls buckle. A glimpse of water blasting in –

The lights go out. Complete darkness . . .

Sound of men screaming barely audible over the sound of blasting water and bending metal –

EXT. DESTROYER — CONTINUOUS

The ship lists, rapidly sinking. The row boats pull away, hard. Gibson prepares to jump – glances back at the closed door to the hold – jumps back, opens the door –

INT. HOLD, DESTROYER — CONTINUOUS

Blackness.

The dim light of the open door becomes a beacon. Tommy spots Gibson waving –

Tommy and Alex claw their way up the steps as the entire ship goes under –

EXT. DESTROYER — CONTINUOUS

Tommy and Alex burst free of the door as it sinks beneath the waves and –

They pull away from the disappearing ship with the strength born of absolute desperation . . .

Cut to:

EXT. MOONSTONE, ENGLISH CHANNEL — DAY

George hears planes behind them. He looks up –

Three Spitfires in confident formation sweep overhead . . .

Mr Dawson keeps his eyes on the black smoke ahead of them.

> MR DAWSON
> Spitfires, George. Greatest plane ever built.

George smiles. Then looks quizzical –

> GEORGE
> You didn't even look.

MR DAWSON

Rolls Royce Merlin engines. Sweetest sound you could hear out here.

INT. CABIN, MOONSTONE – CONTINUOUS

Peter is folding a chart. A clicking sound catches his attention – the handle of the forepeak door is being rattled from the other side. Peter freezes, uncertain what to do . . .

BANG *– the rattles become bangs–*

SHIVERING SOLDIER
(*out of shot*)

Hello?! Anyone there?!

Peter puts the chart down, takes a step towards the door –

BANG!

SHIVERING SOLDIER
(*out of shot*)
OPEN UP, DAMMIT!

Peter freezes. Turns back to the companionway –

EXT. MOONSTONE – CONTINUOUS

Peter pokes his head out. Mr Dawson looks at him, quizzical –

PETER

He wants to come out –

The banging and shouting of the Shivering Soldier continues.

MR DAWSON

What did you do? Lock him in?

Peter is at a loss.

Let him out, for God's sake!

INT. CABIN, MOONSTONE – CONTINUOUS

Peter comes down the companionway, reluctantly approaching the banging, rattling door . . .

The banging stops . . .

Peter reaches up to the bolt, braces, gently slides it back . . .

Opens the door. The forepeak is empty . . . Peter rushes in, spots the open forward hatch . . .

EXT. MOONSTONE, CONTINUOUS

Mr Dawson leans down to try and see in the cabin –

> SHIVERING SOLDIER
> (*out of shot*)
> You haven't turned around!

Mr Dawson turns calmly to the Shivering Soldier.

> MR DAWSON
> No. We have a job to do.

> SHIVERING SOLDIER
> Job? This is a pleasure yacht! You're weekend sailors, not the bloody navy! A man your age –

> MR DAWSON
> Men my age dictate this war. Why are we allowed to send our children to fight it?

> SHIVERING SOLDIER
> YOU SHOULD BE AT HOME!

> MR DAWSON
> There won't be any home if we allow this slaughter across the Channel. There's no hiding from this.

Cut to:

INT. COCKPIT, SPITFIRE 1 — DAY

Farrier chases the 109 as it circles around on Collins ...

INT. COCKPIT, SPITFIRE 2 — DAY

Collins glances out at his burning wing. Checks his altimeter, checks his canopy is locked in the half-open position –

Lower ...

INT. COCKPIT, SPITFIRE 1 — CONTINUOUS

Farrier fires at the 109, chasing him off –

> FARRIER
> He's turned tail, I'm after him –

INT. COCKPIT, SPITFIRE 2 — CONTINUOUS

Collins checks his belts are tight, checks the release pin on his harness –

> COLLINS
> Good luck. Watch your fuel ... (*Reads.*) Fifteen gallons.

Checks his Mae West, puffing into the inflating tube –

Lower ...

INT. COCKPIT, SPITFIRE 1 — CONTINUOUS

Farrier grease pencils the reading on the chart –

> FARRIER
> Fifteen gallons, understood ...

INT. COCKPIT, SPITFIRE 2 – CONTINUOUS

FARRIER
(*over radio*)
Best of luck, Collins.

Collins checks wind direction, checks wave direction on the surface of the water –

Lower . . .

Turns, lining up along the the waves as he descends . . .

Lower . . .

The water rushes by blindingly fast . . .

INT. COCKPIT, SPITFIRE 1 – DAY

Farrier watches Spitfire 2 carve gracefully across the water, before coming to a stop, floating.

Farrier spots a civilian yacht heading for Collins . . .

He sees Collins' hand stick out of the canopy, waving . . . He tips his wings at Collins, turns away, looks ahead, chasing the 109 towards Dunkirk . . .

Cut to:

EXT. WATER, JUST OUTSIDE DUNKIRK HARBOUR – NIGHT

Tommy and Alex, life jackets on, swim on the swell, bodies and burning wreckage all around, fuel burning on the surface of the water.

Tommy and Alex pull for an overloaded row boat. Tommy grabs the side, tries to climb. He's pushed off by the men inside –

MALE VOICE
Piss off – it's too crowded!

Alex is grabbing at the rail as well –

ALEX

You can't leave us! Make some room –

SOLDIER
(*out of shot*)
You men, leave off. You'll capsize the boat – it's gone over twice on the way out here . . .

Tommy looks at the Soldier. It is the Shivering Soldier, not yet shivering, in full control of his faculties.

SOLDIER

You have to stay calm. There are plenty of boats.

ALEX

Calm?! Wait till you get torpedoed, then tell us to be calm!

SOLDIER

You have life jackets?

MALE VOICE

Yeah, they do.

SOLDIER

Don't panic, the water's not too rough, or too cold. We're heading back to the beach –

MALE VOICE

Fuck off! Let's go to Dover!

Several voices join in.

SOLDIER

We can't make it across the Channel on this, lads. We need to get back to the beach and wait for another ride. (*Gestures.*) It's not even half a mile. You men in the water float here, save your strength, we'll come back for you.

The men start rowing.

Gibson is in the back. Alex spots him.

Gibson quietly drops the rear painter (a small rope attached to the stern) into the black water.

44

Alex takes it, hands part of it to Tommy and they quietly drag behind the boat as it rows in to the shore . . . The men in the rear notice, but nobody says anything . . .

As the dawn breaks, the small, packed boat pulls across the calm water to the vast, packed beach at Dunkirk.

Cut to:

EXT. MOONSTONE – DAY

The Shivering Soldier steps up to Mr Dawson –

> SHIVERING SOLDIER
> What is it you think you can do out there?! On this thing?!

> MR DAWSON
> Not just us. The call went out – we won't be the only ones to answer.

> SHIVERING SOLDIER
> YOU DON'T EVEN HAVE GUNS!

> MR DAWSON
> Did you have a gun?

> SHIVERING SOLDIER
> Course. A rifle – 303.

> MR DAWSON
> Did it help you against the dive bombers? Or the U-boats?

The Shivering Soldier glares at Mr Dawson.

> SHIVERING SOLDIER
> You're an old fool. And you're going to die if you don't turn around.

The booms echo. Closer now.

> SHIVERING SOLDIER
> We're turning around, now!

The Shivering Soldier steps towards Mr Dawson, screaming at the top of his lungs –

SHIVERING SOLDIER
TURN IT AROUND! TURN IT AROUND! –

Peter, hearing this, makes his way back from the bow. The Shivering Soldier grabs the wheel. George grabs his shoulder –

The Shivering Soldier smashes his elbow into George's face, sending him flying backwards down the companionway –

Peter pulls the Shivering Soldier away from the wheel.

PETER
Calm it down, mate.

The Shivering Soldier looks at him, shocked. Confused.

Peter calls down the companionway –

PETER
George?

Nothing.

PETER
George?!

Nothing. The Shivering Soldier watches as Peter climbs down to find –

INT. CABIN, MOONSTONE – CONTINUOUS

George, sprawled out at the foot of the steps, on his back, quietly groaning, bleeding from the back of the head. Peter grabs a life jacket and puts it behind George's head.

PETER
It's okay. You're okay. It's okay.

George blinks at Peter. Frightened.

Cut to:

INT. COCKPIT, SPITFIRE I – DAY

Farrier chases the 109, gradually closing . . .

Up ahead, a convoy of ships is gathered around the entrance to the harbour . . .

Farrier passes over a fishing trawler with a blue cabin, covered with soldiers, strangely low in the water, water washing across its decks . . .

He looks up ahead to the 109, just coming into range . . .

He spots German planes in the distance, heading towards him – he sights the 109 . . . Fires a short burst . . . Nothing . . .

He remembers his fuel gauge . . . Pointlessly pushes the button next to the cracked gauge.

No response.

Farrier checks his position on his chart. Checks the last fuel reading he grease-penciled . . . knows he should turn around –

Farrier sights the 109, banking slightly to bring it across his sights . . .

Farrier fires – the 109 starts smoking, dropping –

Farrier spins around – turning away from the approaching planes. Heading for Dover . . . for home.

As he passes over the sinking blue trawler, he sees men jumping into the water, swimming for a destroyer nearby . . .

In his rear-view mirror: the enemy planes approaching . . .

Farrier looks at his cracked fuel gauge . . . Thinking . . .

Cut to:

EXT. BEACH AT ZYDECOTE (7 MILES EAST OF DUNKIRK) – DAWN

The surf has picked up since yesterday . . .

Tommy, Gibson, Alex lie on the beach, sleeping as the light comes up on a stormy day.

In the distance, towards the dark smoke of Dunkirk, the lines of men extend into the sea.

Nearby, small groups of soldiers attempt to climb onto small vessels. Row boats are being swamped and overturned in the surf, overcrowded boats are grounded on the sand –

MALE VOICE
Right. Three of you out, or the rest's stuck.

Soldiers give up their places. Some head back out of the surf. Some wade out past the break . . .

EXT. BEACH AT MALO LES BAINS – CONTINUOUS

Colonel Winnant walks the beach, surveying. He approaches a group of Engineers driving trucks onto the sand, taking the air out of their tires, laying duckboards on top . . .

ENGINEER
(*brightly*)
A pier. When the water comes back in. Tide's turning, now.

Colonel Winnant looks out at the churning water.

COLONEL WINNANT
How can you tell?

ENGINEER
(*quietly*)
The bodies come back.

48

Colonel Winnant looks out at the water – men in line, chest deep, gently push floating bodies aside as they wash in.

EXT. BEACH AT ZYDECOTE – CONTINUOUS

Tommy bangs a tin of vegetables on a rock. It springs a leak and he sucks the juice. Gibson holds out his hand. Tommy keeps sucking for a beat or two, then hands it over.

Tommy watches Vanquisher loading troops from the vast crowd lining the mole. Despairing.

Alex opens his eyes and sits up. Spots some Highlanders walking past, away from Dunkirk in loose formation . . .

> ALEX
> Hey! Highlanders!

Tommy watches as Alex gets to his feet, heading over to his regimental comrades.

> ALEX
> What's that way?

> HIGHLANDER 1
> (points)
> A boat.

Alex follows his gesture to a fishing trawler with a blue cabin, listing in the shallows a mile up the beach.

> ALEX
> She's grounded.

> HIGHLANDER 2
> Not when the tide comes in, she isn't.

Tommy and Gibson are already on their feet. Alex nods at them as they follow the Highlanders down the beach towards the grounded trawler . . .

Cut to:

INT. CABIN, MOONSTONE – DAY

Peter goes down below to check on George. He checks the
bleeding on the life jacket behind George's head.

>   PETER
> What'd you want to come along for, George?

>   GEORGE
> Sea cadet? You and Mr Dawson? Best thing I ever done.
> Only thing I ever done. I told my dad I never done nothing
> at school. I told my dad I'd do something one day. Maybe
> get in the local paper.

>   PETER
> The *Herald*? Why?

>   GEORGE
> Maybe teachers would see it. Make my school proud.

>   PETER
>   *(laughs)*
> Who cares what your bloody school thinks, George?

George looks up at Peter, desperate.

>   GEORGE
> Please! Please don't laugh at me!

Peter looks at George, deciding how to respond.

>   PETER
> I'm going to laugh at you, George – cos you're being
> bloody silly.

George is crying.

>   PETER
> Now, stop it. I need you back up on deck.

George keeps crying.

GEORGE

I can't. I can't see.

Peter looks at him. Gets a blanket, puts it across George's chest.

PETER

Get some rest.

Peter gets up. Looks down at the softly weeping boy.

I'll need you as soon as you're able.

George nods. Smiling through his tears.

EXT. MOONSTONE, ENGLISH CHANNEL – DAY

Peter comes up on deck.

The Shivering Soldier, crouched in the well, stares at him. Mr Dawson is at the helm. Peter comes close. Speaking low –

PETER

The blood won't stop. Should we turn back?

Mr Dawson looks back towards Britain. Then forward to France. Thinking. Shakes his head.

MR DAWSON

Come too far.

BOOM! Explosions nearby –

The Shivering Soldier moves into a foetal position.

Mr Dawson and Peter look ahead to where plumes of water rise, seemingly in slow motion, amongst the ships up ahead. German bombers drifting overhead, 109 fighters buzzing around them . . .

Mr Dawson holds his course . . .

Cut to:

INT. COCKPIT, SPITFIRE I – DAY

Farrier flies, distracted, glancing from his broken fuel gauge to the switch for his reserve fuel tank . . .

>   FARRIER
> Sod it.

Farrier banks, coming around . . .

Farrier climbs, trying to gain advantage for the coming encounter, lining up on the German planes threatening the destroyer and the blue trawler . . .

Cut to:

EXT. BASE OF THE MOLE – CONTINUOUS

Colonel Winnant makes his way towards the crowded mole. Stretchers of French troops are brought down to the mole. A Private comes out of the crowd, breathless.

>   PRIVATE
> The French've been forced back on the western side, sir.

Colonel Winnant looks at explosions over the warehouses.

>   COLONEL WINNANT
> But they're still holding a perimeter?

>   PRIVATE
> For now.

Colonel Winnant pushes on down the mole . . .

EXT. THE MOLE – MOMENTS LATER

He finds Bolton, but no ships . . .

>   COLONEL WINNANT
> Where're the destroyers?

COMMANDER BOLTON

There'll be one soon.

COLONEL WINNANT

One?

COMMANDER BOLTON

After yesterday's losses, it's one ship on the mole at a time.

COLONEL WINNANT

The battle's here, what're they saving them for?

COMMANDER BOLTON

The next battle. The one for Britain. Same with the planes.

COLONEL WINNANT
(*peers through his field glasses*)

But it's right there! You can practically –

COMMANDER BOLTON

Seeing home doesn't help us get there, Captain.

Colonel Winnant turns to the flaming town at their backs.

COLONEL WINNANT

They need to send more ships, dammit! Every hour the enemy pushes closer.

COMMANDER BOLTON

They've activated the small vessels pool –

COLONEL WINNANT

Vessels pool?

COMMANDER BOLTON

The list of civilian boats for requisition –

COLONEL WINNANT

Civilian? We need destroyers.

COMMANDER BOLTON

Small boats could load from the beach.

Colonel Winnant watches men struggling to load in the surf.

COLONEL WINNANT
Not in these conditions.

COMMANDER BOLTON
I'd rather face waves than dive bombers.

Colonel Winnant looks up at the cloudy sky –

COLONEL WINNANT
You're right – they won't get up in this . . .

COLONEL WINNANT
(*points*)
The Royal Engineers are building piers from lorries –
should help when the tide comes back.

COMMANDER BOLTON
We'll know in six hours.

COLONEL WINNANT
I thought tides were every three?

COMMANDER BOLTON
Then it's good that you're army and I'm navy, isn't it?

*Colonel Winnant allows himself a smile. Commander Bolton
spots a shape on the horizon.*

COMMANDER BOLTON
Vanquisher . . .

Cut to:

EXT. MOONSTONE, ENGLISH CHANNEL – DAY

*Mr Dawson, at the helm, studies the horizon. Peter joins him,
glaring at the Shivering Soldier before taking a seat.*

Mr Dawson hears something, starts scanning the sky . . .

Spots a distant plane . . . Peter follows his gaze.

*Mr Dawson throws the wheel, bearing to starboard, hard,
throttling up –*

Heinkel.

Mr Dawson points at a minesweeper heading towards them . . .

They'll go for the minesweeper.

Shouldn't we stand by? To pick up survivors?

To do that we have to survive ourselves.

As the boat motors away, Peter looks back to see the Heinkel and its two fighters moving towards the minesweeper . . .

Cut to:

EXT. GROUNDED TRAWLER – DAY

The Highlanders approach, cautiously. The beach is deserted here – just disabled army vehicles and dead bodies . . .

The blue trawler is tilted towards them. They circle the hull, checking it . . . it seems sound enough.

Tommy and Gibson follow the Highlanders as they climb up onto the abandoned trawler . . .

EXT. DECK OF GROUNDED TRAWLER – CONTINUOUS

Tommy looks over at the dunes above them. Alex looks around the boat, turns to Highlander 1.

Where's the crew?

Probably got spooked after they ran aground. Scarpered up the beach.

ALEX

Why?

HIGHLANDER 2

We're outside the perimeter. Enemy could be right there –
(*Points at the dunes.*) Best shut ourselves inside and wait
for high tide . . .

Highlanders heads down the companionway into the small hold.

ALEX

How long's that?

HIGHLANDER 3

Every three hours.

They descend into the hold, shutting the door behind them.

Cut to:

EXT. MOONSTONE, ENGLISH CHANNEL – DAY

As the Moonstone *ploughs through the swell, Peter looks back
at the Heinkel coming over the minesweeper . . .*

Peter spots –

PETER

Spitfires! Dad, Spitfires!

*Mr Dawson turns to see two Spitfires diving at the German
bomber and its fighter escort. One Spitfire dives right between
two 109s, setting one alight.*

He got him, he got him!!

*The other Spitfire flies close over the Heinkel, which turns away
from the ship. Mr Dawson eases back on the speed . . .*

MR DAWSON

The Heinkel's moved off . . .

As they watch, one of the Spitfires starts smoking . . .

PETER

Oh, no.

Mr Dawson sees the smoke, throws the wheel, spinning the yacht around to head back –

MR DAWSON

Watch for a parachute!

Mr Dawson throttles up . . .

Cut to:

INT. COCKPIT, SPITFIRE I – DAY

Farrier hears his engine skip a beat, puts his gloved finger on the reserve tank toggle switch, listening . . . His engine evens out again. He puts his hand back on the stick, focusing on the German planes . . .

He throttles up, speeding into the fray, climbing . . .

Cut to:

INT. HOLD, GROUNDED TRAWLER – DAY

Dimly lit by a couple of small, dirty portholes.

The soldiers lie around the hold. Sleeping or chatting. Alex is scrounging around the hold, finding nothing useful.

ALEX
(to Gibson)

Poke your head out, see if the water's coming in.

Gibson shakes his head, pulling his arms tight around himself. Alex glares at him –

Talkative sod.

Tommy gets up, climbs up to the door, cracks it. Crawls up into the well – peeks over the rail –

The boat is in inches of water.

>   TOMMY
> Bugger. Barely come in at all.

>   ALEX
> For fuck's sake.

>   HIGHLANDER 3
> Calm down. What goes out comes back in, right?

>   ALEX
> Yeah, but how long?

Silence answers this. Clearly no sailors aboard.

Cut to:

EXT. MOONSTONE, ENGLISH CHANNEL — DAY

The Moonstone *pushes through the swell, full speed, diesel engine straining . . .*

Peter watches the smoke-trailing Spitfire fly lower and lower . . .

>   PETER
> No parachute . . .

Mr Dawson is watching the plane like a hawk, steering around the waves by instinct . . .

INT. COCKPIT, SPITFIRE 2 — CONTINUOUS

The water flashes by blindingly fast . . .

Collins pulls back on the stick, raising the nose as the plane –

Hits the water with a jolt and a tearing sound. Collins thrashed against his belts, forward/back/left/right –

Bang –

EXT. MOONSTONE – CONTINUOUS

Peter watches the Spitfire 'land' on the surface of the water –

PETER

He's down.

INT. COCKPIT, SPITFIRE 2 – CONTINUOUS

*With a shooosh, the plane is floating over the swell, like a
sprinter hearing the gun. Collins releases his belts, starts
inflating his life vest, pulls the catch on the canopy, yanking it
back along its track. It jams . . . He thrusts his hand through the
gap, struggling . . . From outside it looks like he is waving . . .*

*He looks up to see Farrier's Spitfire shoot over, dipping a wing
in salute . . .*

*Collins sits in the gently bobbing plane, collecting himself as he
watches the water start to rise around the slowly sinking plane.*

Collins tries the canopy again –

Jammed.

He is trapped in the sinking plane . . .

Cut to:

INT. COCKPIT, SPITFIRE 1 – DAY

Farrier levels off, looking down at the Heinkel approaching –

It has a single fighter escort – an ME 109 off the port wing . . .

Cut to:

INT. HOLD, GROUNDED TRAWLER – DAY

*Tommy jolts awake – there are steps outside. He moves up to
the door. Highlander 1 gets his rifle, moves in front of the door.
Aims. Nods at Tommy . . .*

59

Tommy throws open the door. A Seaman stands there –

SEAMAN

Nee, nee!

Highlander 1 is confused.

Tommy grabs the Seaman, pulling him down into the hold. Highlander 1 holds his gun on him –

ALEX

Kraut?

The Seaman looks uncomprehendingly up at Alex –

ALEX

Are you German?!

SEAMAN

Dutch! Dutch! Merchant navy. Here to pick you up. To help you.

They sit him up.

ALEX

Why'd you leave your boat?

SEAMAN

In case Germans come. We wait up the beach with the soldiers. Wait for the tide.

HIGHLANDER 2

You came back, the tide must be in.

SEAMAN

Coming, yes. But more hours till we float.

ALEX

Hours?! Why'd you come back?

The Seaman gestures around the packed hold –

SEAMAN

Not so heavy when I left!

Alex and the others take this in.

A gunshot penetrates the hull – everybody lies flat, Tommy stares at the bullet hole, which lets in light . . .

Cut to:

EXT. MOONSTONE, ENGLISH CHANNEL – DAY

Mr Dawson pushes the boat towards where the plane went down.

> PETER
> There was no 'chute, dad . . .

Mr Dawson ignores him. The engine is screaming . . .

> PETER
> Dad, there was no 'chute. He's probably dead –

> MR DAWSON
> (*snaps*)
> Damn it, he might be alive!!

Peter is shocked at his dad's outburst.

Mr Dawson stares at where the plane went down . . .

Cut to:

INT. COCKPIT, SPITFIRE I – DAY

Farrier lines up for his attack . . . Sighting the Heinkel as it commits to its bombing run over the destroyer, Farrier pushes forward on his stick, going into his dive . . .

Cut to:

INT. HOLD, GROUNDED TRAWLER – DAY

Everybody stares at the bullet hole, not making a sound . . .

Another shot punches a hole two feet from the first –

Highlanders near the holes ease away, squeezing up against other soldiers . . .

BANG! A third shot, directly above the first . . .

Two Highlanders grab their rifles, going for the stairs –

> TOMMY
> No! Then they'll know we're in here.

> HIGHLANDER 1
> Why else are they shooting at us?!

> TOMMY
> Look at the grouping . . .

Everybody looks at the three bullet holes.

> TOMMY
> Target practice.

BANG! A fourth hole, near the others . . . Cut to:

EXT. MOONSTONE, ENGLISH CHANNEL – DAY

The Moonstone is getting closer to the Spitfire bobbing on the waves.

Close enough to see that it is sinking . . .

> MR DAWSON
> Peter, go forward with the boat hook.

INT. COCKPIT, SPITFIRE 2 – CONTINUOUS

Collins smashes the canopy back and forth on its track . . . Jammed, jammed, jammed.

Water starts pouring in, streaming through the gap in the half-open canopy. He shuts it . . . Trapped . . . Opens it, yanking, water pouring in . . .

Collins searches around looking for inspiration, for an implement, for anything –

Water rising past his ankles . . . his calves . . .

Cut to:

INT. COCKPIT, SPITFIRE 1 — DAY

Farrier dives, plummeting towards the Heinkel . . .

He glances across at the 109, which suddenly banks towards him, clearly reacting to Farrier's attack . . .

Cut to:

INT. HOLD, GROUNDED TRAWLER — DAY

As the men stare at the bullet holes, water starts slopping through the lowest ones . . . A Highlander goes to plug the holes

BANG! The Highlander screams, clutching his face. His comrades pull him back, trying to smother his cries . . .

The water pours in steadily through the lowest holes. Alex points at the target zone —

ALEX

We have to plug it!

HIGHLANDER 2

After you, mate!

They stay back from the holes, wary. Watching the water pour in . . .

Cut to:

INT. COCKPIT, SPITFIRE 2 — DAY

Collins pulls the steel flare gun from its holder. Water is coming up over his legs now . . . He smashes the flare gun into the canopy, again and again . . .

Cut to:

INT. COCKPIT, SPITFIRE I – DAY

Farrier fires at the Heinkel. Tracers zipping at the bomber. The 109 rises at him, guns blazing. Farrier rolls away, trying to dodge the fire –

EXT. SKY ABOVE DUNKIRK HARBOUR – DAY

As Spitfire 1 rolls away, the Heinkel releases its load – bombs falling around the destroyer –

Cut to:

INT. HOLD, GROUNDED TRAWLER – DAY

A burst of machine-gun fire opens a new group of holes beside the first –

Alex watches the water spraying in. He turns to the Dutch Seaman –

ALEX
How do we get off?! Do we need to ditch some ballast?!

The Dutch Seaman looks at him, uncomprehending –

ALEX
Weight! Do we need to lose weight!

The Dutch Seaman shrugs.

SEAMAN
Weight, yes.

Alex turns to face the group –

ALEX
Somebody needs to get off.

HIGHLANDER I
Well volunteered.

64

                              ALEX

We don't need a volunteer. I know someone who ought
to get off . . .

Alex turns to Tommy and Gibson. Points at Gibson.

                              ALEX

This one. He's a German spy.

                             TOMMY

Don't be daft.

Alex stares Gibson down . . .

                              ALEX

He's a bloody Jerry. You might not've noticed that he
hasn't said a word, but I have. He doesn't speak English –
or if he does it's with an accent thicker than sauerkraut
sauce –

                             TOMMY

You're daft. Tell him.

Gibson just stares at Alex . . .

                              ALEX

Yeah, tell me.

*Nothing. Just the sound of water spraying in hard, jetting in
through the bottom holes . . .*

Cut to:

INT. COCKPIT, SPITFIRE 2 – DAY

*Collins smacks the canopy. The flare gun bounces off. He drops
the flare gun, scrambles to find it under the water. The water is
rising up his chest . . .*

Cut to:

INT. COCKPIT, SPITFIRE 1 – DAY

Farrier cuts right, dodging away from the 109 –

Banking hard, he gets a clear look at the destroyer weathering the explosions.

A plume of water right next to the destroyer comes so high he flies through the top of its spray.

Cut to:

INT. HOLD, GROUNDED TRAWLER – DAY

Alex turns to Highlander 1, holds out his hand for his gun. Highlander 1 hands it over. Alex moves at Gibson, pointing the rifle, hooks the barrel on Gibson's tags, pulling them closer to read –

> ALEX
> Tell me . . . Gibson!

Tommy looks at Gibson, panicking –

> TOMMY
> Tell him, for God's sake!

Alex pushes the rifle against Gibson's cheek. Gibson cracks –

> GIBSON
> FRANÇAIS! JE SUIS FRANÇAIS!

Tommy stares, shocked. Alex moves back slightly, taking this in.

A burst of machine-gun fire. Everyone ducks from ricochets.

> ALEX
> A Frog. A bloody Frog. A cowardly little queue-jumping Frog . . .

With the end of his rifle Alex shakes Gibson's tags –

ALEX

Who's Gibson, eh? A naked dead Englishman lying out on that sand. Or did you at least have the decency to bury him?

'Gibson' just stares.

TOMMY

He did. I helped him. I thought it was his mate.

ALEX

Maybe he killed him –

TOMMY

He didn't kill him –

ALEX

How do we know?!

TOMMY

How hard is it to find a dead Englishman on Dunkirk beach, for God's sake?! He didn't kill anyone – he was looking for a way off the damned sand like the rest of us!

The water is spraying in from more and more holes as the water level rises . . .

Alex has the rifle on Gibson. Another burst of machine-gun fire.

HIGHLANDER 2

Haven't they had enough practice by now?!

HIGHLANDER 1

They're making sure she won't float.

Highlander 2 looks at the holes spraying water, the water pooling in the bottom of the hold. He turns to the Seaman –

HIGHLANDER 2

Will she still float?!

The Seaman assesses the leaks . . .

SEAMAN

Float, yes. With less weight, yes –

ALEX

And we know who's getting off –

TOMMY

You can't do that. We're on the same side.

Alex nudges Gibson with the rifle –

ALEX

Go on, up you go –

TOMMY

As soon as he pokes his head out they'll slaughter him –

ALEX

Better him than me –

TOMMY

It's not fair –

ALEX

Survival's not fair.

HIGHLANDER I

No, it's shit. It's fear and greed. Fate squeezed through the bowels of men. Shit.

TOMMY

He saved our lives.

HIGHLANDER 2

And he's about to do it again – Go on –

Alex starts shoving Gibson up the stairs.

TOMMY

No! Just stop!

Alex turns to Tommy, looks him in the eye –

ALEX

We need someone to get off so the rest of us can live – You
want to volunteer?

TOMMY

Fuck no. I'm going home.

ALEX

And if this is the price?

TOMMY

I'll live with it, but it's wrong.

Alex shoves Gibson up another step, opens the door –

TOMMY

Alex, one man's not going to make enough difference –

HIGHLANDER 1

You'd best hope it does, cos you'd be volunteering next –

TOMMY

What?

ALEX
(indicates Highlanders)
We're regimental brothers, mate. Just the way it is.

*Gibson grabs for the rifle. Tommy jumps at Alex to help
Gibson. They smash against the hull – as they drop into the
water, the ship levels –*

SEAMAN

FLOAT! WE FLOAT!

HIGHLANDER 2

START THE BLOODY ENGINE!

The Seaman is already crawling out the hatch, reaching up –

The engine starts, loud as loud can be –

*Machine-gun fire strafes the hull. The men duck below the
waterline . . .*

The Seaman throws the screw into reverse, full throttle . . .

The men hold their breaths under the water at the bottom of the hold as bullets pepper the hull . . .

Cut to:

INT. COCKPIT, SPITFIRE 2 – DAY

Collins, water up to his ears now, grabs the flare gun – swinging underwater less effective.

Now he panics, pushing his face up against the canopy, banging with his fists, instinct taking over, no more thought, no more plan – banging, banging, water rising over his ears. Smash – something cracks into the canopy right above his head. He recoils. It impacts the canopy again, smashing a hole –

It is a boat hook . . .

Collins pulls himself through the hole, elbows first, forcing himself through, pushing off his seat, underwater, he pushes up from the sinking plane . . .

EXT. WATER, JUST OUTSIDE DUNKIRK HARBOUR – CONTINUOUS

Collins breaks the surface, gasping, looks around –

A private yacht with a young man on the bow, boat hook extended . . .

Collins grasps the boat hook.

COLLINS
(*breathless*)

Afternoon.

Cut to:

INT. COCKPIT, SPITFIRE 1 – DAY

Farrier comes around again, searching the sky for the German planes . . .

He looks down at the destroyer. It is leaking oil from a large hole in its side . . .

The dark oil slick spreads quickly across the water, covering the men in the water between the trawler and the destroyer . . .

Cut to:

EXT. THE MOLE — DAY

The destroyer Basilisk *casts off. Men cover every available piece of deck.*

Commander Bolton watches her wake. Colonel Winnant approaches –

>   COLONEL WINNANT
> We've wasted the day, Commander.

>   COMMANDER BOLTON
> I share your frustration, Colonel.

They hear distant shots –

Commander Bolton raises his field glasses . . . He sees a blue trawler stuck in the shallows miles down the beach.

>   COMMANDER BOLTON
> Grounded trawler, taking fire.

Colonel Winnant takes the field glasses . . .

>   COLONEL WINNANT
> The enemy's breaking through the dunes to the east. This is it.

INT. HOLD, GROUNDED TRAWLER — DAY

Tommy comes up for air, gasping, spluttering . . .

Water is pouring in from dozens and dozens of holes . . .

Alex comes up, coughing, with Gibson . . .

ALEX
We're off!

Alex crawls over to the stairs, climbs out into the well –

EXT. TRAWLER – CONTINUOUS

Alex pokes his head out as the Seaman is sneaking up to see where they are headed –

The Dutch Seaman turns the wheel, jumps back onto the floor of the well as bullets impact the cabin. He throws the engine into forward gear, turns to Alex –

DUTCH SEAMAN
THE HOLES! PLUG THE HOLES!

Alex crawls back downstairs –

INT. HOLD, TRAWLER – CONTINUOUS

Alex falls down the stairs –

ALEX
PLUG THE HOLES! PLUG THE HOLES!

The men stuff rags, bolts, fingers, anything they can lay hands on to plug as many holes as possible . . .
Cut to:

INT. CABIN, MOONSTONE – MOMENTS LATER

Collins, drying himself with a blanket, looks down at George, whose breathing is shallow, sightless eyes open.

COLLINS
(*to Peter*)
I don't really know, son. You were right not to move him. (*Reassuring.*) You've done the best for him you can.

EXT. MOONSTONE, WATER OUTSIDE DUNKIRK HARBOUR — CONTINUOUS

The Shivering Soldier watches Collins come out on deck –

> SHIVERING SOLDIER
> Is he alright?

> PETER
> (*out of shot*)
> No.

Peter is glaring at the Shivering Soldier.

> PETER
> No, he's not –

BOOM! Collins follows Mr Dawson's gaze to a destroyer up ahead being bombed by a Heinkel, huge plumes of water rising just beside her . . .

The Shivering Soldier retreats into himself. Peter runs up to the bow –

A blue fishing trawler a quarter of a mile off, sinking . . .

> PETER
> Dad, there's men in the water!

Mr Dawson looks ahead to where Peter is pointing. He puts the throttle forward, heading into the fray . . .

Collins spots Spitfire 1 arcing around, trying to get a bead on the Heinkel . . .

> COLLINS
> Come on, Farrier . . .

Cut to:

INT. COCKPIT, SPITFIRE 1 — DAY

Farrier pulls on the stick, lining up behind a 109 . . .

He fires, chasing down the plane, firing again . . . Smoke from the German plane, which starts to drop . . .

Farrier is in a heavy dive, when his engine chokes.

Farrier's hand darts forward, switching to his reserve tank before the engine can die . . .

The engine catches again. Farrier pulls out of the dive . . .

Cut to:

EXT. THE MOLE – DAY

Through the binoculars Colonel Winnant watches the blue trawler pushing out to sea, low in the water . . .

Commander Bolton watches a destroyer, under full steam, heading out to the Channel . . .

Where there are shapes of boats on the horizon . . .

EXT. DECK OF TRAWLER – CONTINUOUS

The Dutch Seaman aims the boat at a destroyer out at the mouth of the harbour . . .

EXT. HOLD, TRAWLER – DAY

Tommy, Gibson, Alex, Highlander 1 and the others stuff the holes as best they can. The makeshift plugs pop out every few seconds – the soldiers scrabble under water to find them and stuff them back in, hands pressed against water jets, spray coming in everywhere . . . *

EXT. THE MOLE – CONTINUOUS

Omitted.*

* In previous drafts of the script, this is the point at which Bolton and Winnant first see the Little Ships. Ultimately in the cutting room, they returned the entrance of the Little Ships to this location in the film.

EXT. DECK OF TRAWLER — CONTINUOUS

The Dutch Seaman looks over the rail, concerned, to see how fast his boat is lowering into the swell . . .

Cut to:

EXT. MOONSTONE, WATER OUTSIDE DUNKIRK HARBOUR — DAY

Collins watches Farrier spin around to get after the Heinkel.

The Moonstone comes up on the men in the water. Collins comes to the side, to help Peter fish men out, notices the surface of the water –

> COLLINS
> (to Mr Dawson)
> Oil. We're getting into oil!

Mr Dawson puts the screw into reverse, stopping the boat.

They fish men out of the water – the men covered in oil, anonymous in their glossy black filth . . .

Cut to:

INT. COCKPIT, SPITFIRE I — DAY

Farrier chases down the Heinkel, closing in as its top turret opens up on him, tracer fire lighting up all around him –

He dives down under the range of the rear turret, then angles up, firing at the bomber's tail . . .

Cut to:

EXT. BLUE TRAWLER — DAY

The Dutch Seaman sees water sloshing over the deck.

ABANDON SHIP! ABANDON SHIP!

INT. HOLD, TRAWLER — CONTINUOUS

The soldiers, holding back the water, cannot hear him . . . One by one they start to abandon the task. More and more water pouring in . . . Alex and Gibson are last – Alex turns, sees they are alone, grabs Gibson by the shoulder then jumps for the exit. Gibson, still holding back the water, notices too late –

EXT. BLUE TRAWLER — CONTINUOUS

Tommy gets on deck, sees the Keith, *a quarter of a mile away. He dives into the water, pulling away from the swamped trawler –*

All the men dive off the sinking boat, swimming for the Keith.

INT. HOLD, TRAWLER — CONTINUOUS

Gibson dives for the exit. He is blasted back by water, dragged down with the sinking trawler . . .

Cut to:

EXT. MOONSTONE, WATER OUTSIDE DUNKIRK
HARBOUR — DAY

Peter, Collins and the first oil-covered men pull more oily men from the water, the decks of the yacht rapidly filling. Mr Dawson looks at the oil slick, concerned. He addresses the oily survivors –

MR DAWSON

Below deck.

OILY SURVIVOR

No fear.

MR DAWSON

We need to get as many of you on board as we can before the oil catches fire. Get below or get off my boat – your choice.

The oily survivors head below decks. Peter runs back to the companionway to shout down –

PETER

Careful there!

INT. CABIN, MOONSTONE – CONTINUOUS

Peter pokes his head down, sees two oily survivors moving George from the bottom of the steps –

PETER

Careful!

The oily survivors look up at him. Alex is one of them –

ALEX
(*quiet*)

He's dead, mate.

Peter takes this in . . .

PETER

So be bloody careful with him!

EXT. THE MOLE – CONTINUOUS

Commander Bolton stares at the shapes in the distance . . .

He grabs the field glasses from Colonel Winnant, puts them to his eyes –

Boats. Civilian boats. All shapes and sizes. An armada.

Colonel Winnant peers over Commander Bolton's shoulder . . .

77

COLONEL WINNANT

What can you see?

Commander Bolton slowly lowers the glasses.

COMMANDER BOLTON
(*gentle*)

Home.

Colonel Winnant grabs the glasses, confused . . .

EXT. DECK OF A DESTROYER – CONTINUOUS

The soldiers peer over the railing at the absurd collection of vessels passing them in the opposite direction:

Yachts, paddle steamers, fishing trawlers, day sailers, ferries, dredgers, dinghies, row boats . . .

Crewed by:

Fishermen, merchant navy sailors, naval officers, civilian crew, naval crew, nurses, retired sailors . . .

The exhausted soldiers lining the decks of the Basilisk *start to clap, then to cheer . . . Some are crying . . .*

EXT. MOONSTONE, WATER OUTSIDE DUNKIRK
HARBOUR – CONTINUOUS

Peter steps out of the cabin, reeling. Meets his dad's questioning glance with unmistakable shock –

SHIVERING SOLDIER
(*out of shot*)

The lad . . .

Peter turns. The Shivering Soldier is looking up at him with terrified eyes, blanket tight around his shoulders.

Will he be okay?

Peter looks at the Shivering Soldier. Sees the white knuckles clasping the edge of the rough blanket. Peter nods.

The Shivering Soldier turns, staring out at the destroyer.

Peter catches Mr Dawson looking at him. Approving.

Collins, pulling a man from the water, looks up at Spitfire 1 chasing down the Heinkel –

> COLLINS
> Come on, Farrier . . .

Cut to:

INT. COCKPIT, SPITFIRE 1 – DAY

Farrier strafes the Heinkel – *no apparent effect*. Zipping over it, he dives down out of range of its turret, banks hard left to line up for another shot. A 109 cuts across him, Tracer fire shooting past.

Cut to:

EXT. WATER, JUST OUTSIDE DUNKIRK HARBOUR – DAY

Tommy swims for the Keith . . .

He hears an airplane . . . looks up to see a Heinkel coming in over the Keith . . . The bombs drop, plumes of water shoot upwards all around the ship. Tommy dives under the water for protection. The explosions are deafening – he holds his ears with his hands –

Tommy breaks the surface. The barrage is over, the Keith is still afloat. Tommy swims for it. Getting closer, Tommy realizes he's swimming in oil, the black sludge covering his head and arms. He looks back – the blue trawler is gently slipping beneath the water . . .

Tommy makes for the Keith, even as he sees men jumping into the water from her decks, lifeboats being lowered . . .

Tommy spots another craft – a yacht heading towards them.

Tommy pulls for the yacht as hard as he can . . .

Cut to:

EXT. BEACH AT MALO LES BAINS – CONTINUOUS

The rag-tag collection of small ships works the beach, picking men up in the shallows, ferrying them out to bigger ships . . .

Small open boats use the truck 'pier' to load men as the Engineer looks on with pride . . .

EXT. MOONSTONE, WATER OUTSIDE DUNKIRK HARBOUR – DAY

The Moonstone *is filled with oil-covered men, throughout the hold and across the decks – many more still in the water . . .*

The Keith *lists, men jump off the far side, away from the oil slick, where small ships are gathering to pick them up . . .*

Collins moves up the side, watching Farrier bank hard to get behind the Heinkel. A 109 zips across his path, guns blazing . . .

Collins looks down at the oil-covered water . . .

INT. COCKPIT, SPITFIRE I – CONTINUOUS

Farrier pulls around, hard. The Heinkel is in front of him, side on, heading in for another run at the Keith.

Farrier banks and pulls up to keep the bomber in his sights as he fires his cannons –

The Heinkel catches fire and starts falling . . .

EXT. MOONSTONE, WATER OUTSIDE DUNKIRK HARBOUR – CONTINUOUS

Collins sees the Heinkel catch fire – turns to Mr Dawson.

GO! GO! GO!

Mr Dawson throws the engine into gear, turns the wheel –

The Heinkel falls flaming towards the oil slick . . .

Peter has hold of one last oil-covered survivor, who hangs on for dear life as the boat drags him through the oily water –

The men left in the water shout with despair as the Moonstone *motors away –*

The flaming Heinkel hits the water – explodes –

The surface of the water catches fire, spreading across the water. Men duck underwater to escape the flames.

Underwater: Highlander 1 pushes down under, looking up at the fire. The surface is aflame as far as he can see . . .

Peter holds on to the oil-covered soldier –

Who is now being washed with cleaner water as they come out of the slick. As the oil comes off his face we see that it is Tommy . . .

Collins watches, appalled, as the men in the water are engulfed by relentless flames . . . The Keith *is going down – survivors on the far side are picked up by the various small ships . . .*

Under the water, Highlander 1's air runs out. The flames rage above . . .

His instinct to breathe pushes him up into the flames where he is engulfed, screaming, dying –

Tommy lies on the deck at Peter's feet, eyes closed . . .

TOMMY
(*a whisper*)

Take me home.

Cut to:

INT. COCKPIT, SPITFIRE 1 – DAY

Farrier sees the Heinkel explode, turns away towards the beaches . . .

He looks down at –

The thousands of men on the beach.

The small ships ferrying out to the larger vessels.

The narrow mole with its endless rope of men . . .

Farrier is awestruck . . .

He hears his engine start to sputter . . .

It dies and the prop stops . . .

EXT. THE MOLE – CONTINUOUS

Commander Bolton watches with satisfaction as a paddle steamer ties up. He calls up to a Stewardess (fifty-nine) –

COMMANDER BOLTON

Where're you from?

STEWARDESS

Out of Dartmouth!

Bolton shakes his head in joyous disbelief. He watches men load into a small open sailboat crewed by two young men.

COMMANDER BOLTON

From Deal?

They nod.

Mind the current at the mouth, boys.

Bolton spots Spitfire 1. It soars overhead. He waves –

MALE VOICE
(*out of shot*)
Where've you been all my life?!

Commander Bolton sighs at this . . . then notices. No engine noise.

He watches the Spitfire, concerned, until –

Hears something – another engine . . . A high whine . . . He turns to see –

A Stuka . . .

The men lining the mole shift restlessly. Trapped . . .

Cut to:

EXT. MOONSTONE, ENGLISH CHANNEL – EVENING

The Moonstone *chugs along, low in the water, men laying down along her decks . . .*

INT. CABIN, MOONSTONE – CONTINUOUS

Men lie on every available space, packed in like sardines. Tommy catches sight of Alex looking at him. Tommy nods.

EXT. MOONSTONE, ENGLISH CHANNEL – CONTINUOUS

Mr Dawson is at the helm. Collins hears a distant engine –

COLLINS
That's a fighter –

MR DAWSON
ME 109, from the South. Peter, take the wheel, listen for my instructions.

Mr Dawson steps up onto the seat to look above the roof of the cabin . . .

Point her south.

Peter turns the wheel, the Moonstone *swings to port, straightens up. Mr Dawson spots the 109, closing . . .*

Cut to:

EXT. THE MOLE — DAY

Commander Bolton turns to see the Stuka approaching, its distinctive kinked-wing silhouette bearing down like an awful bird of prey . . .

The soldiers stir, some crouching, some closing their eyes. Commander Bolton takes a knee, bracing. He bites his lip as the Stuka goes into its dive, that terrible whine building . . .

Cut to:

EXT. MOONSTONE, ENGLISH CHANNEL — EVENING

Mr Dawson stares at the approaching 109 –

> MR DAWSON
> Full speed ahead.

Peter throttles up –

The 109 is growing close now . . .

> MR DAWSON
> Get ready to pull hard to port . . . Before he fires he'll have to lower his nose, I'll give you the signal . . .

Peter reaches over to the side of the wheel, ready to throw it. The 109 is practically upon them . . .

Cut to:

EXT. THE MOLE — DAY

Commander Bolton is mumbling a prayer as he watches the Stuka come at them –

BLAM BLAM BLAM BLAM BLAM!!

The Stuka is strafed with fire as Spitfire 1 flashes past –

INT. COCKPIT, SPITFIRE 1 – CONTINUOUS

Farrier darts past the Stuka, gliding, guns blazing . . .

EXT. THE MOLE – CONTINUOUS

The Stuka never fires, it just smashes into the sea . . . The soldiers all along the mole cheer.

INT. COCKPIT, SPITFIRE 1 – CONTINUOUS

Farrier watches the Stuka disintegrate on the surface of the water. He nods . . . feeling the unaccustomed silence . . .

Cut to:

EXT. MOONSTONE, ENGLISH CHANNEL – EVENING

Mr Dawson stares at the approaching 109. Peter glances back and forth between the 109 and his father . . .

> MR DAWSON
> Wait for it . . . wait till he's committed to his line . . .

The nose of the 109 dips down –

> MR DAWSON
> NOW!

Peter throws the wheel, the Moonstone *lurches to port –*

The guns on the 109 light up, strafing the water to starboard –

The 109 flashes over . . . Collins watches it recede.

> COLLINS
> He's off.

> MR DAWSON
> Bigger fish to fry.

85

Collins looks at Mr Dawson. Curious.

> COLLINS
> How'd you know all that, anyway?

Mr Dawson steps onto the deck.

> MR DAWSON
> My son's one of you lot. I knew he'd see us through.

Mr Dawson moves forward. Collins steps up beside Peter.

> COLLINS
> You're RAF?

> PETER
> Not me. My brother. Flew Hurricanes. He died third week into the war.

Collins looks forward at the proud father standing by the mast.

Cut to:

INT. COCKPIT, SPITFIRE I – DAY

Farrier sits in the silence, gliding . . . looking to see how far he might make it up the beach . . .

Cut to:

INT. CABIN, MOONSTONE – EVENING

Tommy gets to his feet, steps over other men as he slips over to the stairs . . .

EXT. MOONSTONE, ENGLISH CHANNEL – EVENING

Tommy and Alex poke their heads out –

> PETER
> Stay below, please.

                                    TOMMY
    We just want to see the cliffs –

Tommy looks over at white cliffs, ghostly above the dark water.

                                    TOMMY
    Dover?

Peter shakes his head, amused.

                                    PETER
    Weymouth.

Alex shakes his head, sadly.

                                    ALEX
    We let you all down, didn't we?

Peter just looks at this exhausted, ragged boy his own age.

Cut to:

INT. COCKPIT, SPITFIRE 1 – DAY

*Farrier glides, banking, looking for a suitable stretch of beach
to ditch . . .*

*In the strangely silent plane, he passes over the troops, lines up
on the vast stretch of sand beyond Malo les Bains . . .*

Cut to:

EXT. HARBOUR AT WEYMOUTH – NIGHT

*Soldier after soldier climbs out of the yacht. The Corporal
handing out travel chits marvels at the absurd amount . . .*

                                    CORPORAL
    How many you got in there?

The Shivering Soldier is taken ashore, wrapped in blankets.

*Tommy and Alex stick together as they are handed hot cups of
tea and shepherded out of the harbour in long lines.*

Peter supervises as George's body is taken ashore.

As Collins steps off the boat a soldier from another boat spots his RAF uniform –

> SOLDIER
> (*furious*)
> Where the hell were you!

Collins just stands there. He feels a hand on his shoulder. It is Mr Dawson. He indicates the men filing off the Moonstone *–*

> MR DAWSON
> They know where you were.

Mr Dawson puts his hat on. To go home.

EXT. WEYMOUTH RAIL YARD – NIGHT

Tommy and Alex, exhausted, downcast, are herded across the tracks towards a train. Before getting on they are handed a blanket and cup of tea by an Elderly Man, who looks at their hands, not their faces, as he hands the rough blanket over –

> ELDERLY MAN
> Well done, lads . . . well done, lads . . .

> ALEX
> All we did is survive.

> ELDERLY MAN
> That's enough. Well, done, lads, well done, lads . . .

Alex steps up onto the train. The Elderly Man reaches out to Tommy, touching his face – clearly blind.

INT. TRAIN – CONTINUOUS

Tommy flops down, lying across the seat. Alex is slumped opposite, tears starting to roll down his cheeks.

> ALEX
> That old bloke wouldn't even look us in the eye.

No response. He looks over. Tommy is already asleep.

Cut to:

EXT. THE MOLE – EVENING

The mole is empty but for bodies.

A Private opens his eyes. He sits up, alone on the deserted mole, his comrades gone, mistaken for dead . . .

> COMMANDER BOLTON
> (out of shot)
> Come on, then, Private . . .

The Private looks down at the water to see Commander Bolton standing in a launch full of army officers.

> COMMANDER BOLTON
> I know we're officers, but it's us or the enemy, so now's not the time to be particular . . .

The Private scrambles down into the launch, where Colonel Winnant stands talking to Commander Bolton.

They look out at the vast deserted beach, littered with corpses and abandoned equipment . . .

> COLONEL WINNANT
> (to Commander Bolton)
> Churchill got his thirty thousand.

> COMMANDER BOLTON
> And then some. Almost three hundred thousand. So far.

Commander Bolton steps back up onto the mole.

> COLONEL WINNANT
> So far?

> COMMANDER BOLTON
> I'm staying. (Off look.) For the French.

The launch pulls away from Commander Bolton on the mole.

Cut to:

INT. TRAIN – MORNING

*Sunlight flickering on Tommy's eyelids wakes him. We have the
sense that he has been asleep for a very long time.*

*The train full of soldiers rolls to a halt. Alex opens the window,
spots a Boy near the tracks –*

> ALEX
>
> Hey! Where are we?!

> BOY
>
> Siding. You'll pull in in a minute –

> ALEX
>
> What station?

> BOY
> (*surprised*)
>
> Woking.

Alex spots stacks of newspapers waiting to be loaded.

> ALEX
>
> Grab me one of them papers.

The Boy hesitates.

> Go on!

*The Boy pulls the paper off the top and stretches up to hand
it to Alex. Alex slumps into his seat. The headline:*

> CHURCHILL ADDRESSES DUNKIRK EVACUATION
> IN COMMONS

Alex thrusts the paper at Tommy.

> ALEX
>
> I can't bear it. You read it.

                    TOMMY
Can't bear it?

                    ALEX
They'll be spitting at us in the streets. If they're not locked
up waiting for the invasion.

Cut to:

EXT. WEYMOUTH TOWN – DAY

*Peter walks down the deserted high street. He stops. Walks into
the office of the local paper, the* Herald . . .

INT. HERALD OFFICE – CONTINUOUS

Peter hands the Editor a photograph. Of George.

Cut to:

INT. COCKPIT, SPITFIRE I – CONTINUOUS

*Farrier checks his canopy is locked, stows loose items, pumping
the handle all the while . . .*

EXT. SPITFIRE I – DAY

The landing gear inches out of its housing . . .

Cut to:

INT. TRAIN – DAY

Tommy looks down at the paper. Starts to read. Poorly.

                    TOMMY
'Wars are not won by evacuations.'

Alex shakes his head at this.

The train starts to pull into the station . . .

The platform is crowded with civilians. Alex slinks down into his seat, turning away from the window . . .

A Civilian bangs on the glass, peering in . . .

> **ALEX**
> I can't look.

> **TOMMY**
> 'But there was a victory inside this deliverance which should be noted . . .'

Alex turns. The Civilian grins, holding up two beer bottles. The platform is packed with cheering and waving civilians . . .

Women with sandwiches and drinks rush up to the windows . . .

> **TOMMY**
> 'Our thankfulness at the escape of our army –'

Alex opens the window, grabbing food and drink as Tommy continues to read . . .

> '– must not blind us to the fact that what has happened in France . . . is a colossal military disaster . . .'

INT. COCKPIT, SPITFIRE 1 – DAY

Farrier pumps the handle –

EXT. SPITFIRE – CONTINUOUS

The landing gear inches past halfway down . . .

INT. COCKPIT, SPITFIRE 1 – CONTINUOUS

Pumping the handle, Farrier checks his belts –

> **TOMMY**
> (*voice-over*)
> 'And we must expect another blow to be struck almost immediately . . .'

Farrier holds the plane steady in its descent towards the sands . . .

EXT. BEACH AT LA PANNE – CONTINUOUS

Spitfire 1 swoops onto the flat sand, wheels down.

> TOMMY
> (*voice-over*)
> 'We shall go on to the end, we shall fight in France . . .'

Farrier slides back the canopy and climbs out of the plane . . .

INT. MR DAWSON'S HOME – DAY

Peter, gets up from the kitchen table. Mrs Dawson is at the stove, her back to us.

As Peter grabs his coat he runs into Mr Dawson, letters in hand, looking at the Herald. *He hands it to Peter . . .*

> TOMMY
> (*voice-over*)
> 'We shall fight on the seas and oceans . . .'

The small headline:

> LOCAL BOY, GEORGE MILLS, JUST 17,
> HERO AT DUNKIRK

Peter looks at his father. Nods with satisfaction.

EXT. BEACH AT LA PANNE – DAY

Farrier brushes sand from the wing of his beloved Spitfire . . .

> TOMMY
> (*voice-over*)
> 'We shall fight with growing confidence and growing
> strength in the air . . .'

Farrier pulls his flare gun . . . He shoots into the cockpit . . .

INT. TRAIN – DAY

Alex hangs out of the window, guzzling from a beer bottle, grinning at the women outside . . .

>   TOMMY
> 'We shall defend our island . . .'

Alex turns, deliriously happy, beer running down his chin –

>   ALEX
> What?!

>   TOMMY
>   *(louder, over the celebration)*
> 'We shall defend our island, whatever the cost may be – we shall fight on the beaches, we shall fight on the landing grounds . . .'

EXT. DUNKIRK HARBOUR – EVENING

Bodies gently bob in the water . . .

>   TOMMY
>   *(voice-over)*
> 'We shall fight in the fields and the streets . . .'

Abandoned trucks and anti-aircraft guns, piles of boots, stacks of rifles catch the last light . . .

> 'We shall fight in the hills; we shall never surrender . . .'

Bodies line the length of the mole . . .

> 'And even if, which I do not for a moment believe, this island . . . were subjugated and starving . . .'

EXT. BEACH AT LA PANNE – CONTINUOUS

Farrier kneels, hands on head, as dark shapes of German soldiers (seen only from behind) surround him . . .

TOMMY
(*voice-over*)
'Then our empire beyond the seas, armed and guarded by
the British fleet, would carry on the struggle . . .'

Farrier is led away from the burning plane . . .

INT. TRAIN – DAY

Alex is oblivious. Tommy continues, to himself . . .

TOMMY
'Until, in God's good time . . .'

EXT. BEACH AT LA PANNE – TWILIGHT

Moving towards the burning Spitfire . . .

TOMMY
(*voice-over*)
'The New World, with all its power and might –'

The shape of the plane is still visible beneath the flames . . .

'– steps forth to the rescue and the liberation of the old.'

*Move in on the burning Spitfire until the flames fill the frame
and we –*

Cut to black.

Credits.

End.

Dunkirk

STORYBOARDS

THE MOLE
AND THE HOSPITAL SHIP

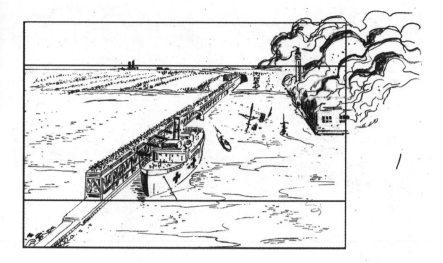

1

21

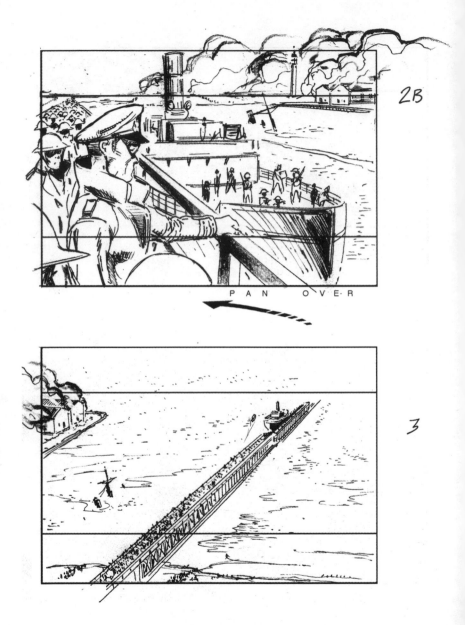

2B

PAN OVER

3

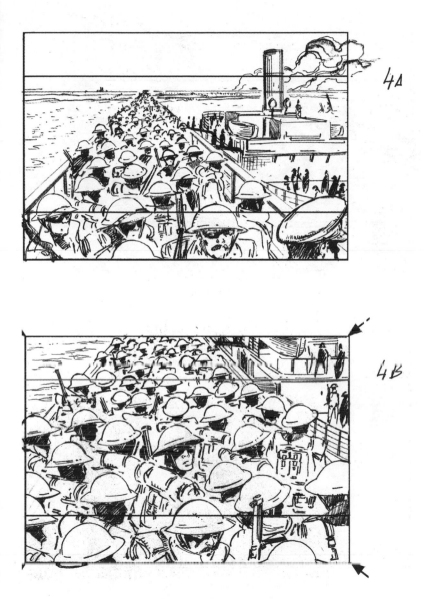

4A

4B

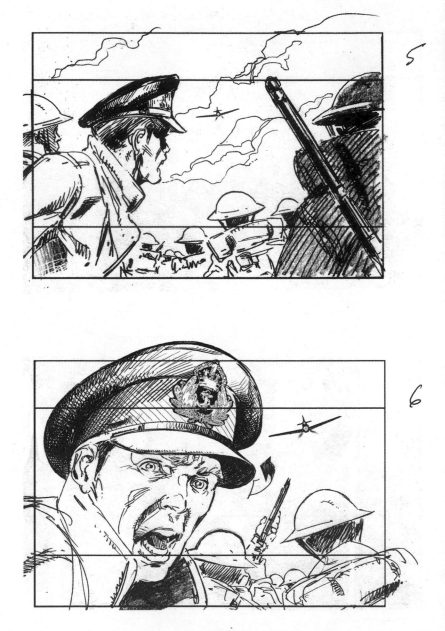

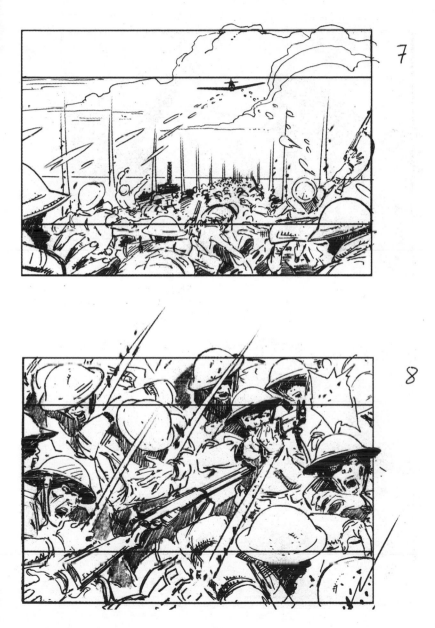

7

8

9

10

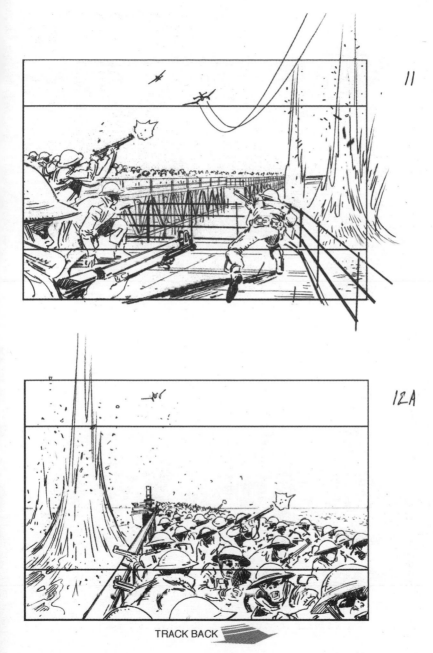

11

12A

TRACK BACK

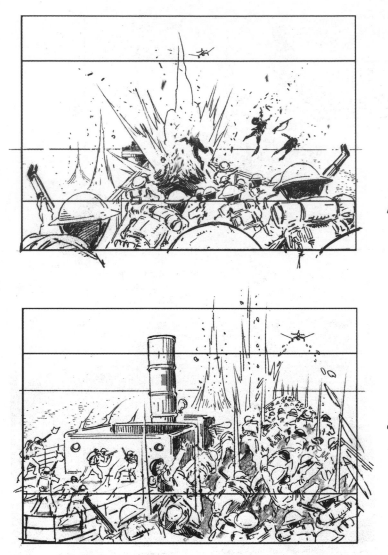

12B

13A

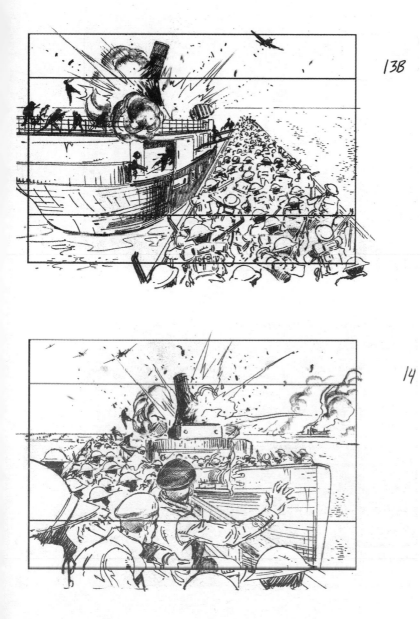

13B

14

15

16

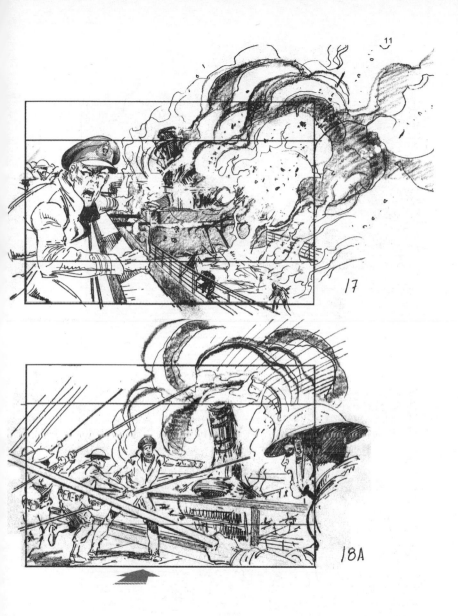

III

18B

19

TOMMY
+
GIBSON

20

TOMMY
+
GIBSON

21

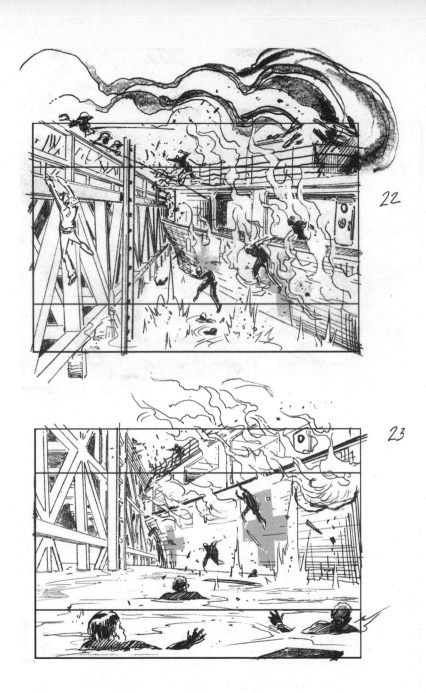

22

23

24

25

26

27

28A

28B

117

28c

29

30

31

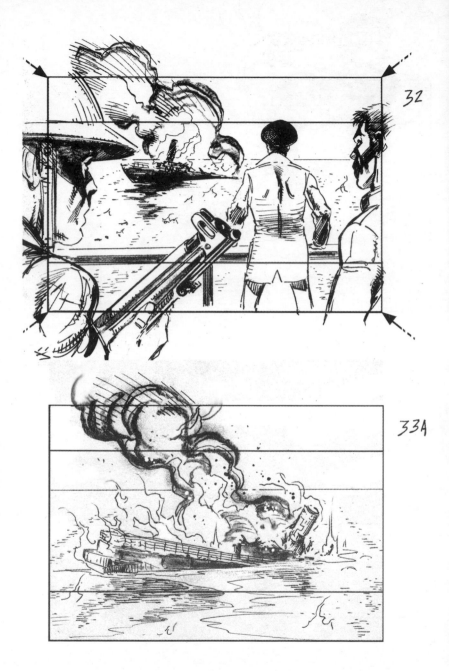

32

33A

33B

CONFLUENCE

SC 142

1

TRAWLER

2

TRAWLER
DUTCH SEAMAN
OTS

3

4

DUTCH SEAMAN
LOOKS DOWN
AT WHERE THEY
ARE — BELOW DECK

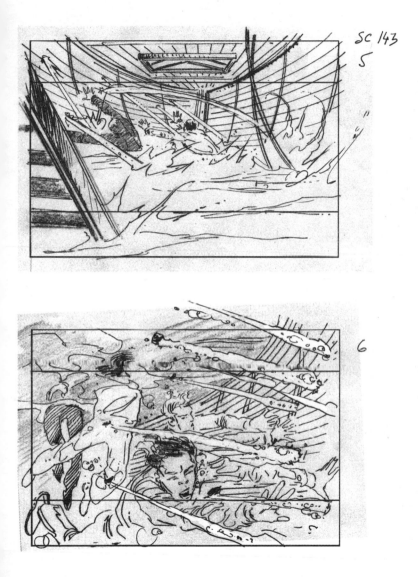

SC 143

5

6

7

SC 144

MOLE / BOLTON

8

9

10

11

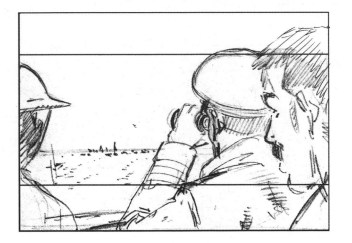

12

13

- 'HOME' -

Sc 145

14 BASILISK
    DECK

15

16

SC 146

17

TRAWLER

18

19

SLIGHTLY TILT UP.

SC 147

BEACH—

20

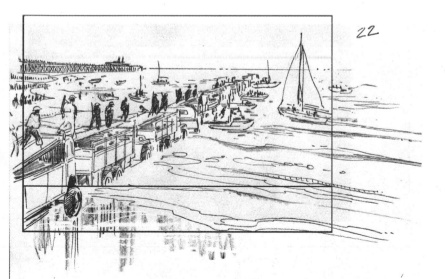

21A

22

23

SC 148

24

PETER

25

26

MR. D

27

MOONSTONE DECK

28

MOONSTONE

C

29

MOONSTONE

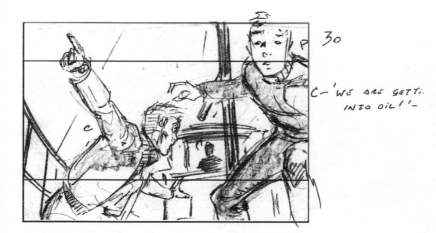

30

C—'WE ARE GETTI.
INTO OIL!'—

31

STOP / REVERSE

32

SLOW DOWN

33

34

COLLINS

PETER

35

36

37

38

SC 149

39

40

144

41

F Low

42

SC 150

TRAWLER

43 A

43 B

146

'ABANDON SHIP! .

44

45

TRAWLER -
BELOW DECK
LOOKING TOWARDS
STERN .

147

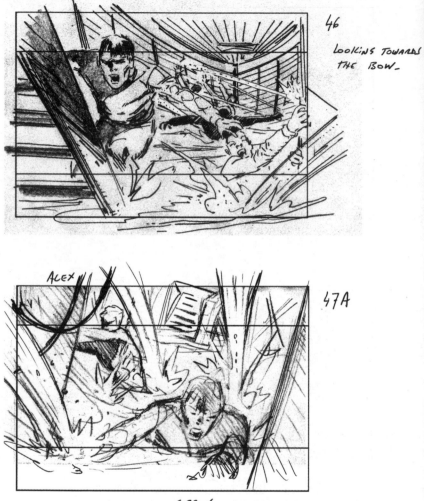

46

LOOKING TOWARDS
THE BOW.

ALEX

47A

GIBSON

148

47B

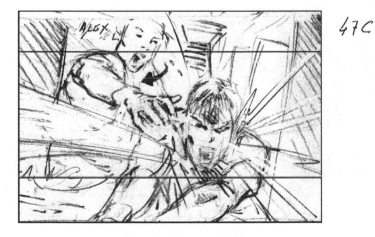

47C

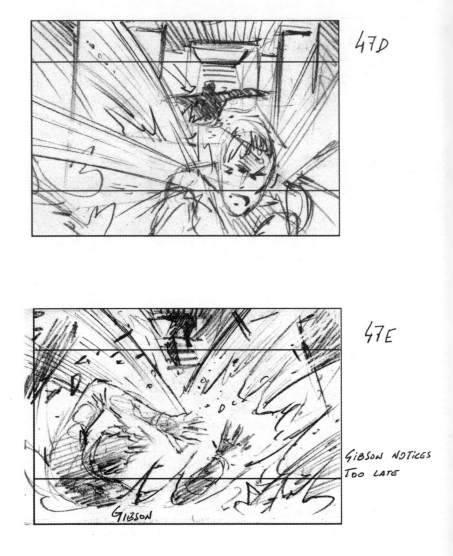

47D

47E

GIBSON NOTICES
TOO LATE

GIBSON

SC 152

48 A

48 B

151

48C

49 A

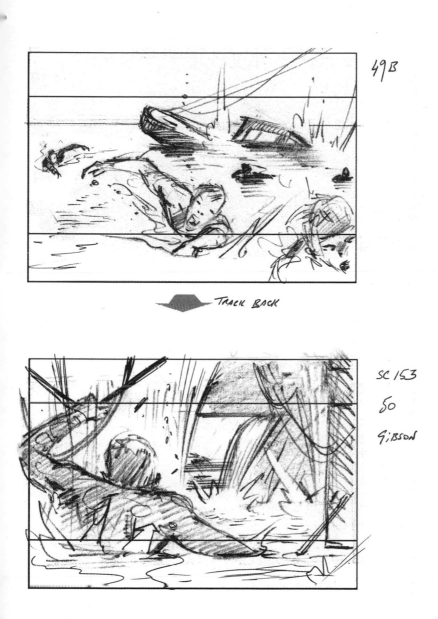

49B

TRACK BACK

SC 153
50
GIBSON

153

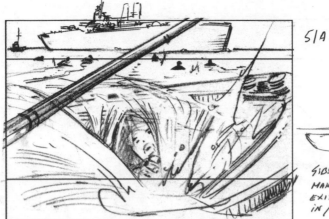

51A

GIBSON BARELY
MAKES IT TO THE
EXIT. WATER RUSHES
IN / HE GOES DOWN —

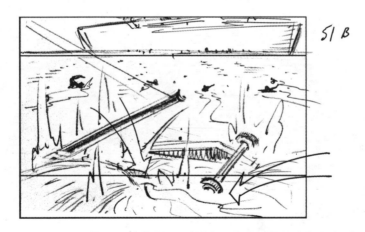

51 B

154

SC 154

52

MOONSTONE　　T R A C K →

53

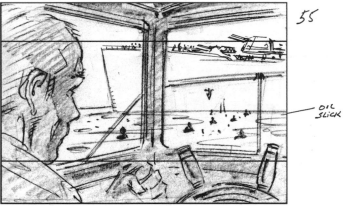

54

DAWSON CONCERNED

55

OIL SLICK

MR. DAWSON

56

- 'BELOW DECK' -

57

- 'WE NEED TO GET
AS MANY OF YOU
ON BOARD ...
BELOW DECK OR
OFF MY BOAT.' -

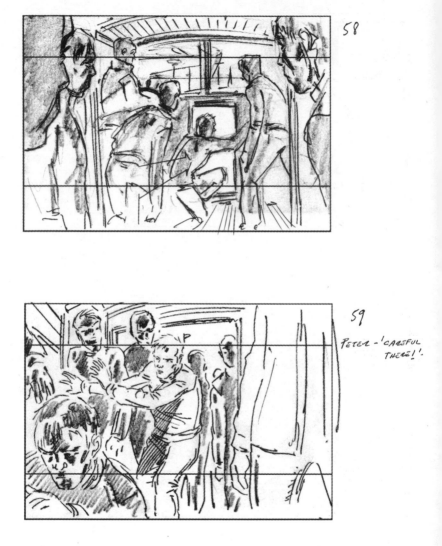

58

59

PETER – 'CAREFUL
THERE!'.

158

SC-155

60

P-'CAREFUL!'-

61

OiLY SURVIVOR
-'HE'S DEAD MATE..'-

159

62

P- 'SO BE BLOODY
CAREFUL WITH
HIM!'—

Sc 156

63

64

DAWSON

SHIVERING SOLDIER
(O.S):
—' THE LAD...'—

PETER·

65 A

D

P

65B

66

162

67

SC 157

68

FARRIER

163

69

FARRIER'S POV

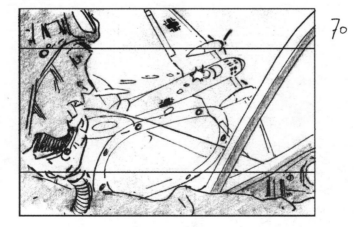

70

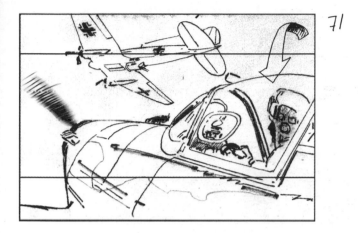

71

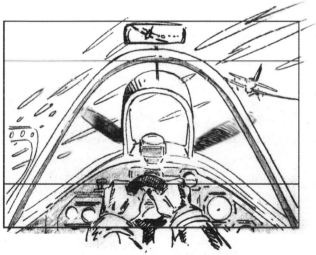

72A

FARRIER'S POV

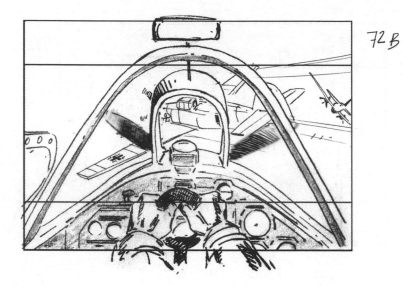

72 B

SC 158

TOMMY

73 A

73B

73C

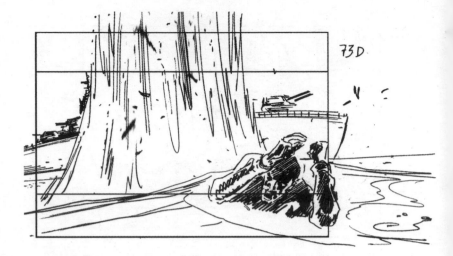

73D

74

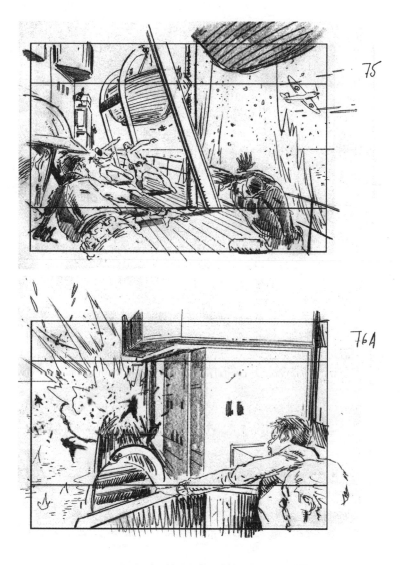

75

76A

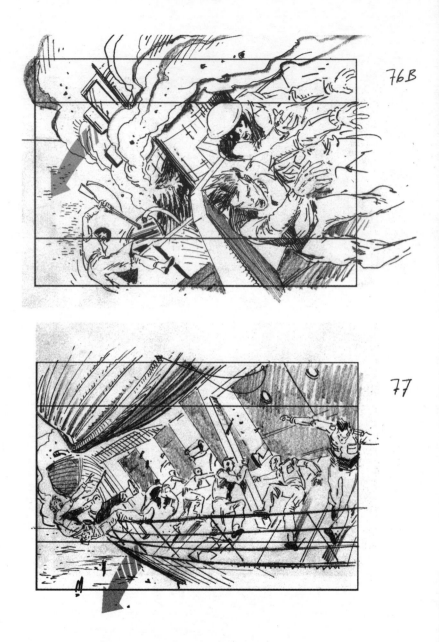

76B

77

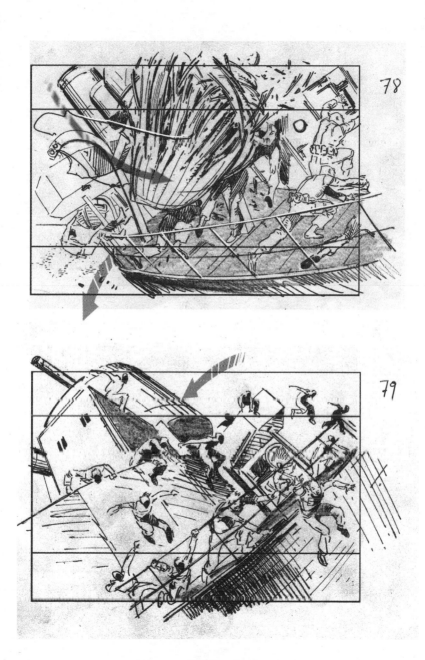

78

79

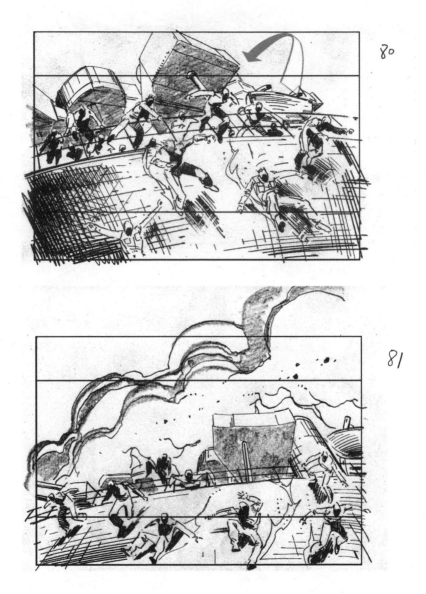

80

81

82

STERN

SC 158 - CONT.

83A

83B

TRACK W/ TOMMY

84A

174

84B

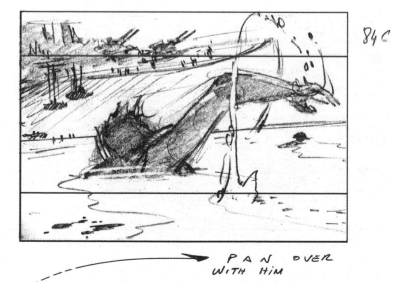

84C

PAN OVER
WITH HIM

175

85

8.6

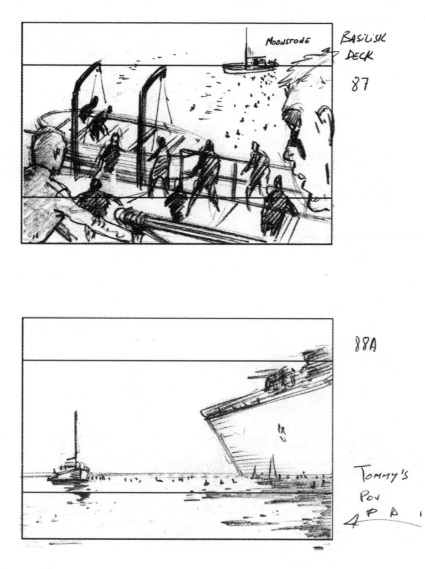

MOONSTONE

BASILISK
DECK

87

88A

TOMMY'S
POV

88B

TOMMY ENTERS
SCREEN SWIMMING
TOWARDS THE
MOONSTONE.

89   SC 159

9/0

COLLINS

9/A

COLLINS' POV

91B

HEINKEL

M-109

FARZER

COLLINS'
TILT UP

92

OIL
SLICK

180

93.

SC 16

9.4

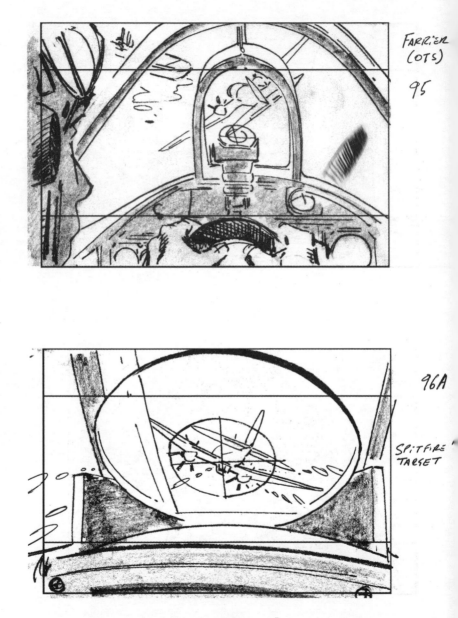

FARRIER
(OTS)

95

96A

SPITFIRE
TARGET

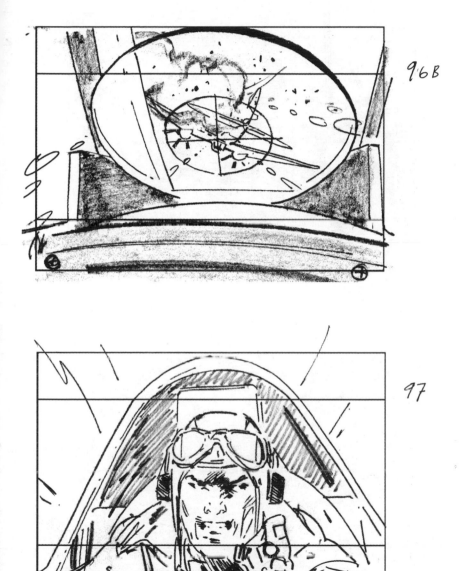

96B

97

MOONSTONE

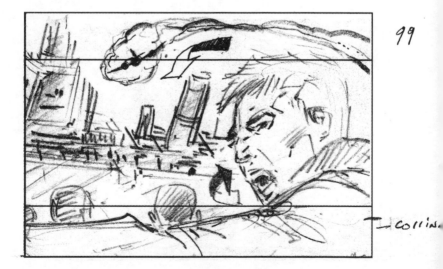

T. COLLIN.

100

COLLINS

MRD

101

102A

102B

186

102C

102D

187

103A

103B

104

105

106

UNDERWAT.

107

HIGHLANDE

108

HIGHLANDER'S
POV

109

COLLINS —

191

/10

COLLINS'
POV

/11

COLLINS'
REACTIO.

192

112

HIGHLANDER 1
RUNNING OUT
OF AIR

113

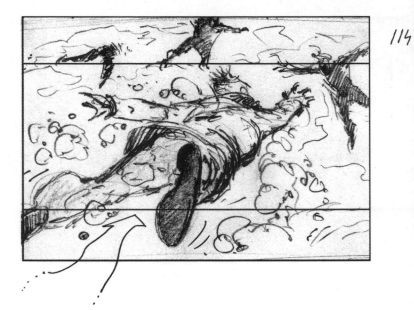

114

11

194

115B

116

PETER   TOMMY

195

117

T-' TAKE ME H

SC-16

118

FARR.

196

119A

119B

120

121